CAPM® 150-Question Sample Exam

By John Tracy

ISBN: 1501017861
ISBN-13: 978-1501017865

This book has been developed as a low-cost alternative 150 question practice CAPM Exam® for those studying for the latest (Summer 2013) version of that exam, as it has changed to accommodate the 5th edition of the *PMBOK® Guide*.

In my years of teaching students preparing for that exam, through several versions of that test, I have noticed clear trends in the *PMBOK® Guide* as it has matured through five editions. I recently had the opportunity to formally review the latest edition and provide feedback as it moved from draft to a published state. I have brought that experience to bear in this practice exam, which is tightly aligned with the CAPM Exam®'s specification in its construction.

The first thing you'll see is a blank answer sheet, which those of you who like to keep your books in pristine condition may use to record your answers. Next comes the test itself. The last section is the test again, this time with the answers appended for each question. This section shows a specific knowledge area and *PMBOK® Guide* reference point to make the process of learning and re-learning easier for you. The book is capped off with a one page summary view of the answers and their associated knowledge area references.

Do not take this exam unless you have read the *PMBOK® Guide*. In fact, you should read it at least twice, and my suggested order of reading is provided in the table below. Please also finish reading this Introduction before investing any more money in this process.

Good luck on your journey. If you have any questions about the material, comments to share, or would like help interpreting your results, feel free to send me an email at jtracli1@gmail.com.

First Reading Sequence: *PMBOK® Guide*	Second Reading Sequence: *PMBOK® Guide*
Chapters 1 – 3	Chapters 1 – 3
Annex A1	Annex A1
Chapters 4 – 10, 13	2 Initiating Processes as listed in P61 Table
Appendix X3	24 Planning Processes as listed in P61 Table
Chapters 11-12	8 Executing Processes as listed in P61 Table
Glossary	11 M & C Processes as listed in P61 Table
Chapter 4 (Re-read, Integration Mgmt)	2 Closing Processes as listed in P61 Table

Deciding to Sit for the CAPM Exam®

In deciding to sit for the CAPM Exam®, there are three hurdles to clear. Please refer to the Certifications Qualifications Table at the very end of this write-up as you read on to see both the PMP® and CAPM® requirements. It's best to consider these hurdles before spending a lot of money.

Since anyone who applies for this exam is certain to have achieved graduation from an accredited high school, the first hurdle is relative to either classroom hours or experience.

If you choose the classroom hours route, twenty-three (23) classroom hours that are project management related are required to sit for the CAPM Exam®. If you do not have 23 classroom hours, you will want to consider signing up for a program. Many are available in differing lengths (anywhere from a week to many months) and modalities (face-to-face, hybrid, online) to meet both your 23 hours requirement and your individualized learning needs. Prices vary from several hundred to several thousand dollars, with online offerings generally being less expensive and more convenient, but also less structured and with less individual attention than face-to-face classes. Note also that there is no time attribute with respect to this requirement, so that project management course you may have taken over 10 years ago is still valid. However, while your classroom hours may be unlimited in life when you apply for the exam, the retention of learning may be much shorter. Therefore, it's best to have a rough idea of your planned exam date before determining the timing of any training program course work.

If you choose the experience route, you'll need to document 1500 hours of experience on a project management team. Regardless of your ultimate choice, think carefully about your relevant work experience before spending money on a learning program.

The second hurdle is what I call the knowledge hurdle. Professional certification exams are typically about demonstrating knowledge and/or experience within the context of the terminology of that profession as laid out by the credentialing body. This exam is no different in that regard. Beginning PMs will have a lot to absorb with the *PMBOK®* *Guide* terminology, but I have seen even seasoned project managers struggle with this over my nine years of teaching in both CAPM® and PMP® programs. Knowing how much you don't know of this terminology (or how much time and work you'll need to map your knowledge to the labels and definitions according to PMI) is important in choosing which type of program – from self-study to an online or face-to-face class, from a one-week cram to a months-long program, or anywhere in between. Leading into the third hurdle, my suggestion in determining what additional help you need is to join PMI, then download and read your free copy of the *PMBOK®* *Guide* (Suggested reading order is provided on the prior page). Once finished, you'll have a much better idea of how much and for how long you'll need to prepare.

The third hurdle is what I call the MAC (Membership/Application/Cash) hurdle. The process of applying to take the exam is in itself a little intimidating for some. My suggestion, noted above, is to become a member of PMI. In addition to providing you a free digital download of the *PMBOK® Guide*, Membership brings you a reduced price for the exam. That $75 difference pays about half of the first year's PMI and Local Chapter membership, and you also gain access to other resources (including some certification exam study materials), monthly/quarterly publications, and a very active networking community. If you are enrolled in a PM learning program, you may also be eligible for a reduced-price membership, which could lower your cash outlay even further.

The Application itself can also be a hurdle for those choosing to enter experience credentials. Some aspirants decide that they don't want to bother, and I believe it is one reason that historically only about 50% of those who enter a pre-certification learning program actually sit for the exam. Many experience gathering spreadsheet forms are available online that make this easier, including the programs in which I teach, so don't sweat this one – it's not as painful as it looks. In fact, if you send me an email, I'll send you my version of that sheet at no additional cost.

Finally, regarding the Cash hurdle, with disciplined self-study, you can do this for less than $400. For example, combined PMI and Local Chapter membership is approximately $150-$160 (less for those qualifying for the student rate). The member exam fee rate is $225, the digital download of the PMBOK is free for members, and the price of this book is less than $10, before shipping costs. For experienced PMs with a good grasp of the PMBOK, this could well be sufficient. However, for those who need more and decide to sign up for a program, even if you don't have a corporate training budget behind you, local workforce programs often have money set aside for such programs – especially if you are between jobs.

Good luck to you on your journey. Feel free to email me at jtracli1@gmail.com if you have any questions.

Certification Qualifications Table

Requirement	PMP Exam® w/ BS/BA	PMP Exam® w/HS Dipl	CaPM Exam® w/HS Dipl
Classroom Hours	35	35	23 (or Experience)
Experience Hours	4500	7500	1500 (or Classroom)
Experience Duration	36 Non-Overlapng Mos	60 Non-Overlapng Mos	No Limit Defined
Experience Interval	Over Last 8 Years	Over Last 8 Years	No Limit Defined

Question	Answer	Question	Answer	Question	Answer
1		51		101	
2		52		102	
3		53		103	
4		54		104	
5		55		105	
6		56		106	
7		57		107	
8		58		108	
9		59		109	
10		60		110	
11		61		111	
12		62		112	
13		63		113	
14		64		114	
15		65		115	
16		66		116	
17		67		117	
18		68		118	
19		69		119	
20		70		120	
21		71		121	
22		72		122	
23		73		123	
24		74		124	
25		75		125	
26		76		126	
27		77		127	
28		78		128	
29		79		129	
30		80		130	
31		81		131	
32		82		132	
33		83		133	
34		84		134	
35		85		135	
36		86		136	
37		87		137	
38		88		138	
39		89		139	
40		90		140	
41		91		141	
42		92		142	
43		93		143	
44		94		144	
45		95		145	
46		96		146	
47		97		147	
48		98		148	
49		99		149	
50		100		150	

Table of Contents

CAPM® 150-Question Sample Exam (3 Hour Time Limit)

1. One key benefit of closing a project or phase is it:

A. Identifies causes of poor processes and validates work meets stakeholder requirements
B. Brings objectivity to the customer acceptance process
C. Releases organizational resources to pursue other enterprise work
D. Documents agreements for future reference.

2. A project charter aligns the project with:

A. The project manager's work priorities
B. The strategy and ongoing work of the organization
C. The project's scope
D. The project management plan.

3. The key benefit of the Close Procurements Process is:

A. It increases the chance of final acceptance
B. It documents agreements for reference
C. It signals that all project activities are complete
D. It provides lessons learned.

4. You are collecting requirements, and feel the need to be creative in your approach. To that end, what techniques could you employ with your team?

A. Regression analysis
B. Unanimity
C. Plurality
D. Affinity diagrams.

5. Factors influencing make-buy decisions include

A. Associated risks
B. Clarity of vendor proposals
C. Outputs of a multi-criteria decision analysis
D. Level of vendor interest.

6. You are concerned with the risk tolerance of a key stakeholder. What is risk tolerance?

A. Level of uncertainty at which that individual will have a specific interest
B. Degree of uncertainty that individual will take on in anticipation of a reward
C. Degree of risk that individual will withstand
D. The value that stakeholder assigns to a specific risk.

7. You are in the midst of doing reserve analysis for your project. Your contingency reserves:

A. Are typically withheld for management control purposes
B. Are associated with the "known-unknowns" for your project
C. Are associated with the "unknown-unknowns" for your project
D. Are not included in the schedule baseline.

8. Techniques for effective communications management include:

A. Nominal Group Technique
B. Observation and conversation
C. Delphi Technique
D. Choice of media and writing style.

9. Disadvantages of virtual teams include which of the following?

A. Exclusion of people with mobility issues
B. Exclusion of projects due to travel expense
C. Possibility of misunderstandings
D. Difficulty including geographically widespread staff.

10. You are exactly midway through a 6-month, $12,000 project with a planned linear spend. You have spent $8,000. What is your CPI?

A. -$2,000
B. Not enough information to determine
C. .75
D. 1.33.

11. The Monitoring & Controlling process group involves:

A. Influencing the factors that could circumvent integrated change control
B. Dealing with any premature project closure
C. Completing the work defined in the project management plan
D. Archiving relevant project documents.

12. Your project sponsor has asked you to shave a week from your project schedule. There are no additional budget dollars to apply, so you decide to fast-track. This means you will likely:

A. Apply overtime
B. Overlap or parallel activities normally done in sequence
C. Accelerate non-critical path activities
D. Reduce scope.

13. Objectives of developing a project team include:

A. Managing conflict constructively
B. Improving project member communications with key stakeholders
C. Improving feelings of trust
D. Selecting the appropriate power type to use in a situational context.

14. You have identified your stakeholders and produced your stakeholder management plan. Now you're proceeding to manage the engagement levels. Process inputs include:

A. Issue logs and work performance data
B. Issue logs and change requests
C. The project charter and project management plan
D. The communications management plan and change log.

15. You are in the process of conducting procurements. What is the key benefit of this process?

A. Aligning internal & external stakeholder expectations
B. Determining the level and type of outside support needed for the project
C. Ensuring seller/buyer performance meet the requirements of the agreement
D. Providing the basis for defining and managing project & product scope.

16. Change requests:

A. Include workarounds
B. Can be formal or informal in nature
C. Include preventive actions and defect repairs
D. Often involve planning for workarounds.

17. You have learned that communications management involves considering the various dimensions of communication. They include:

A. Listening & questioning
B. Encoding & decoding
C. Push & pull
D. Verbal & non-verbal.

18. A colleague is confused about the difference between the project charter and scope statement. You tell him that the scope statement:

A. Contains high level requirements and risks
B. Addresses project exclusions, constraints and assumptions
C. Includes a list of key stakeholders
D. Contains project approval requirements, versus a charter's acceptance criteria.

19. Cause-and-effect diagrams are also known as:

A. Ishikawa diagrams
B. Pareto diagrams
C. Scatter diagrams
D. Histograms.

20. You want to take a structured look at the effectiveness of your risk response strategies. You have therefore decided to:

A. Conduct a variance and trend analysis
B. Hold an all-team meeting to gather input
C. Do a risk reassessment
D. Conduct a risk audit.

21. You have decided on a contract form for your project that allows for reimbursement of all legitimate seller costs, but pays a fee based solely on your subjective determination of seller performance. This contract form is:

A. Time and Materials
B. Cost Plus Award Fee
C. Cost Plus Incentive Fee
D. Cost Plus Fixed Fee.

22. Estimate precision level is critical to understand before making commitments. You have determined your estimate to be in the -25% to +75% range. This is also known as a:

A. Definitive estimate
B. Budget estimate
C. Rough order of magnitude estimate
D. PERT estimate.

23. The integrative nature of project management requires which process group to interact with the others?

A. Planning
B. Executing
C. Integrating
D. Monitoring & Controlling.

24. In analyzing the engagement level of stakeholders, the current engagement levels are compared to desired levels to identify gaps and plans for closing them. Engagement levels for stakeholders include:

A. Unaware, Neutral & Leading
B. Expert, Referent and Legitimate
C. Withdrawing, Collaborating & Compromising
D. Resistant, Supportive & Coaching.

25. Which of the following is true of a definitive estimate (also called grassroots, or engineering estimate):

A. It is generally accurate within plus or minus 10%
B. It is usually based on analogous information
C. It can be prepared quickly
D. It is also called a budget estimate.

26. Techniques for effective management of communications include:

A. Analysis of past performance
B. Push and pull communication
C. Project reports and lessons learned documentation
D. Choice of communications media and facilitation techniques.

27. A RACI Chart:

A. Is a form of an Organizational Breakdown Structure
B. Links the project team members to the work packages
C. Is an acronym that stands for Responsible, Analyze, Consult and Inquire
D. Is not particularly useful in a matrixed project organization structure.

28. Information gathering techniques used in identifying risks include:

A. Force field and multicriteria decision analysis
B. Idea/mind mapping and affinity diagrams
C. Interviewing & Root Cause Analysis
D. Cause-and-effect diagrams and flowcharts.

29. A Project Management Plan:

A. Is generally the same regardless of the complexity of a project
B. Is usually fairly static once put into motion
C. Should be consistent with the program management plan that drives it
D. Includes a section on maintenance of the product of the project.

30. Solution requirements are grouped into:

A. Business & Stakeholder
B. Functional & Non-Functional
C. Quality & Scalability
D. Transition & Project.

31. You are bidding on a project that is potentially very lucrative, but involves some new and highly unstable technology. You decide to proceed with the bid, but also price in some insurance with Lloyds of London in response to the risk level. What type of risk response strategy is this?

A. Mitigation
B. Transference
C. Sharing
D. Enhancement.

32. A Schedule Management Plan includes which of the following?

A. Rules of performance measurement & control thresholds
B. Process to control how change requests will be processed
C. Procedures for project cost reporting
D. A staffing management plan.

33. You are working in the Initiating Process Group. During these processes:

A. The project management plan is developed
B. The strategy and tactics for the project are delineated
C. Project roles and responsibilities are established
D. Internal and External Stakeholders are identified.

34. You have just created a document which includes a set of deliverable acceptance criteria, project exclusions and assumptions & constraints. What is this document?

A. Project Plan
B. Project Requirements
C. Project Scope Statement
D. Work Breakdown Structure.

35. You are planning for your project's procurements. You are likely:

A. Holding a Bidders Conference
B. Doing a Make-or-Buy Analysis
C. Advertising
D. Getting Independent Estimates.

36. Communication Models are important for a project manager to understand in planning communication for their project. As part of the basic communication model:

A. The receiver of the information is responsible for understanding and acknowledging it
B. The receiver of the information is responsible for responding and agreeing to it
C. The complete sequence of model steps is to Transmit, Decode and provide Feedback
D. Noise is not typically an issue.

37. You are in the process of monitoring your project. This involves:

A. Increasing stakeholder support and minimizing resistance
B. Managing communications
C. Measuring and analyzing project performance against the baseline
D. Coordinating the people & resources performing the work.

38. The most common type of dependency relationship found in the Precedence Diagramming Method (PDM), which requires completion of a predecessor before a successor can begin, is called:

A. Finish-To-Finish
B. Start-To-Finish
C. Finish-To-Start
D. Start-To-Start.

39. The term that takes in all prevention/appraisal costs over the life of the product is:

A. Cost of Quality
B. Cost-Benefit Analysis
C. Cost of Non-Conformance
D. Cost of Conformance.

40. A Scope Management Plan includes:

A. Business requirements
B. A process which enables creation of a WBS
C. Quality requirements
D. Training requirements.

41. Inputs used in determining your project budget include:

A. Run Charts & Control Charts
B. Reserve Analysis & Cost Aggregation
C. Risk Register & Basis of Estimates
D. Work Performance Data & Project Funding Requirements.

42. In conducting procurements, a tool used to bring the buyer and potential sellers together prior to proposal submittals is a(n):

A. Proposal pre-evaluation
B. Independent estimate gathering
C. Procurement negotiation
D. Bidder conference.

43. You have just finished your probability & impact assessment and risk categorization. You have a long list of risks. What should you do next?

A. A risk urgency assessment
B. Qualitative risk analysis
C. Quantitative risk analysis
D. Risk response planning.

44. You are debating the benefit of Integrated Change Control with a colleague. He says it's minimizing baseline changes. You think it's:

A. Allowing stakeholders to understand the current project state
B. Ensuring an optimal information flow
C. Allowing for changes to be considered in an integrated manner while reducing risk
D. Providing overall management of project work.

45. Project Management Processes:

A. Ensure the effective life cycle flow of the project
B. Create the project's product
C. Vary by application area
D. Specify the project's product.

46. You are considering techniques to control stakeholder engagement. You choose from:

A. Communication methods, interpersonal skills & management skills
B. Information management systems, expert judgment and meetings
C. Analytical techniques, expert judgment and meetings
D. Stakeholder analysis, expert judgment and meetings.

47. You have a risk that doesn't lend itself to a suitable response strategy. You have decided to establish a budget reserve should it occur. What response strategy is this?

A. Mitigation
B. Passive acceptance
C. Active acceptance
D. Avoidance.

48. Assuming that your team is one that has begun to work together well, has developed a trusting relationship, but has not yet reached its peak output, what stage of development have they reached?

A. Forming
B. Storming
C. Performing
D. Norming.

49. Quality Management and Control tools unique to assurance activities include:

A. Matrix Diagrams & Prioritization Matrices
B. Cause & Effect Diagrams
C. Pareto Diagrams
D. Control Charts.

Use the following data for the next two questions:

You have the following set of six project activities, with associated task durations and predecessor/successor relationships.

A: 2 days; no predecessors
B: 3 days; no predecessors
C: 4 days; both A & B are predecessors
D: 3 days; A is a predecessor
E: 2 days; B is a predecessor
F: 1 day; both C & E are predecessors

50. What is your critical path, and its length?

A. ACF; 7 Days
B. BCF; 8 Days
C. BEF; 8 Days
D. None of the above.

51. More content has been added to Task F, extending its duration to 2 days, and your critical path by one day. To make things worse, your boss has told you that the work must be completed in 6 days, at the lowest possible cost. Looking at the table below, which tasks would you crash, in what sequence, and what would your crashing cost be?

Task	Schedule Days	Crashable Days	Crash Cost/Day
A	2	1	1000
B	3	1	4000
C	4	2	10000
D	3	2	1000
E	2	1	1000
F	2	1	2000

A. D, E & F; $4,000
B. F, E & B; $7,000
C. F, A & C: $13,000
D. F, B & C; $16,000.

52. You are in the process of identifying project risks. Why should you do this?

A. It ensures that risk management is commensurate with the project's importance
B. It enables project managers to focus on high-priority risks
C. It provides the project team the ability to anticipate events
D. It allows the project manager to focus on the right groups of stakeholders.

53. Appendix X3 was added in *PMBOK® Guide* Ed 4, to highlight the importance of a project manager's soft skills. Which of the following skills are on the Appendix X3 list?

A. Trust Building, Conflict Management & Coaching
B. Power, Leadership and Cultural Awareness
C. Facilitation, Motivation & Communication
D. Meeting Management, Decision Making & Negotiation.

54. You have been considering going beyond the simple status report and doing some more elaborate performance reporting for your project. What might you produce?

A. Percent complete report
B. Progress measurements
C. Status dashboards
D. Analysis of past performance.

55. Effective cost control requires:

A. Conducting retrospective reviews & reprioritizing the work backlog
B. Reserve Analysis & Cost Aggregation
C. Influencing change factors and managing them as they occur
D. Ensuring that project outputs meet the requirements.

56. Inputs that may be of particular use to you in controlling your procurements include:

A. Agreements and approved change requests
B. Issue logs
C. Project funding requirements
D. Project schedule.

57. The Qualitative Risk Analysis key benefit is:

A. It ensures that risk management is commensurate with the project's importance
B. It enables project managers to focus on high-priority risks
C. It provides the project team the ability to anticipate events
D. It produces quantitative risk information to support decision making.

58. A resource breakdown structure (RBS):

A. Is a hierarchical list of resources by category
B. Breaks the project's deliverables into work packages
C. Is a hierarchical list of risks organized by categories
D. Shows the project's work organized by work departments.

59. The project charter accomplishes which of the following?

A. Defines how the project is to be executed, monitored, controlled & closed
B. Establishes the project manager's ownership, as its sponsor
C. Authorizes the sponsor to run the project
D. Enables partnering of the performing and requesting organizations.

60. The five Process Groups are:

A. Closing, Executing, Monitoring, Controlling, and Initiating
B. Planning, Closing, Monitoring & Controlling, Managing and Initiating
C. Planning, Closing, Executing, Monitoring & Controlling, and Initiating
D Executing, Monitoring, Controlling, Planning and Initiating.

61. Enterprise Environmental factors affecting the sequencing of a project's schedule activities include:

A. Planning policies, procedures & guidelines
B. Company work authorization systems
C. Schedule network templates
D. Project files from the corporate knowledge base.

62. A Requirements Management Plan includes:

A. Product metrics and a rationale for their use
B. A process that enables creation of a WBS
C. Support and training requirements
D. Acceptance criteria.

63. The stakeholder management plan is:

A. Most effective when widely distributed for comment
B. A document whose key benefit is identifying a stakeholder communication approach
C. A document containing all relevant stakeholder details
D. A sensitive document whose distribution should be limited.

64. Which of the following is true about statistical control processes?

A. Attribute sampling determines whether a result conforms or not
B. Variables sampling defines a range of acceptable results
C. Tolerances identify boundaries of common statistical variation
D. Control limits measure the result on a continuous scale of conformity.

65. You have just finished your risk management plan. What did it likely include?

A. Response strategies & contingency plans
B. Roles & responsibilities, risk process timing & risk categories
C. A list of risks & potential responses
D. A probability of achieving cost & time objectives.

66. A good cost management plan includes:

A. A project organization chart
B. Types of contracts to be used and any potential risk management issues
C. Control thresholds & rules of performance measurement
D. A process specifying how product acceptance will be obtained.

67. You are in the process of executing the project's work. You are:

A. Formally completing the project
B. Planning responses to risk events
C. Measuring and analyzing project performance
D. Coordinating people & resources.

68. A Requirements Traceability Matrix traces requirements for which of the following?

A. Test strategy & scenarios
B. Production support
C. Product scope
D. The WBS.

69. Information considerations to take into account when working in the communications management knowledge area include:

A. Encoding & decoding mechanisms
B. Escalation processes
C. Storage format and manner of retrieval
D. Meeting management techniques.

70. Scope verification & quality control:

A. Are the same
B. Differ, in that scope verification is concerned with deliverables acceptance, and quality control with the correctness of those deliverables
C. Usually happen simultaneously
D. Differ, in that quality control is concerned with deliverables acceptance, and scope validation with the correctness of those deliverables.

71. The Project Management Information System (PMIS):

A. Is the part of organizational process assets providing access to tools
B. Does not include automated gathering methods
C. Is a component of the project management plan
D. Is the part of enterprise environmental factors providing access to tools.

72. You have just finished your Staffing Management Plan. What did it include?

A. Resource calendars & staff release plans
B. A list of project roles & responsibilities
C. Competencies needed to accomplish the project's work
D. A glossary of common project terminology.

73. The key benefit of identifying stakeholders is:

A. Finding out who your stakeholders really are
B. Its impact on keeping scope under control
C. Identifying the right focus for each stakeholder group
D. Its impact on the communication plan.

74. In addition to the seven basic quality management tools and quality management and control tools, an additional quality tool for diagramming pro-anti change degree is the:

A. Pareto diagram
B. Force field analysis
C. Nominal group technique
D. Flowchart.

75. Knowledge Areas include:

A. Scope, Time, Cost & Procurement
B. Quality, Risk, Communication and Planning
C. Integration, Initiating, Stakeholder and Human Resources
D. Scope, Time, Cost & Closing.

76. Early contract termination:

A. Does not require compensation for any work related to the terminated contract part
B. If invoked, gives the buyer termination rights only on the entire contract
C. Results from successful completion of the project
D. Can result from mutual agreement or default of one of the parties.

77. You are trying to decide whether to build or outsource a solution component for a new product expected to generate $300,000 in sales over its life cycle. If you build, it will cost $50,000. If you outsource, it will cost $45,000. You estimate a 5% chance of experiencing customer returns if you build, and 20% if you outsource. Those customer returns would cost you $20,000. Absent of other decision criteria, what is your decision?

A. Build, because $65,000 in estimated costs is less than $70,000
B. Outsource, because $49,000 in estimated costs is less than $51,000
C. Build, because $49,000 in estimated costs is less than $51,000
D. Outsource, because $65,000 in estimated costs is less than $70,000.

78. What is the key purpose for controlling project communication?

A. To effectively engage stakeholders
B. To document the project's approach to ensure efficient communications
C. To ensure optimal communication flow
D. To minimize stakeholder resistance & increase support.

79. You were just in a meeting and heard someone mention something called the "100 percent rule". Immediately after the meeting you pulled up Wikipedia to find out what the term refers to. You found that it means:

A. A Decision Tree accounts for 100% of its event probabilities
B. The work at any WBS level should roll up to higher levels so that nothing is omitted
C. BAC equals 100% of the work to be performed, or 100% of the PVs
D. All of the communication channels on a project need to be accounted for in planning.

80. The Perform Integrated Change Control Process:

A. Begins sometime after the project's inception
B. Accepts changes in both oral and written form
C. Often employs a Change Control Board to review/evaluate changes
D. Requires only the approval of the project manager to move changes forward.

81. You are at the point in your project where you have to begin controlling stakeholder engagement. You are looking through your project plan for information such as:

A. The change management plan, and how human resource requirements will be met
B. Historical information about previous similar projects
C. A description of the organizational culture & political climate
D. Schedules and statements of work.

82. You are working on a project that is projected to take 12 months to complete. The first three months of activity are very well-defined at this point, but the rest of the work schedule looks very hazy to you. What activity definition technique might you use to your advantage in this situation?

A. Joint Application Design
B. Progressive Elaboration
C. Rolling Wave Planning
D. Decomposition.

83. Process groups

A. Will never be conducted within a single phase
B. Are equivalent to project life cycle phases
C. Are typically not reused during the project life cycle
D. Are not project life cycle phases.

84. In using a process to acquire your project team, the key benefit to you is:

A. Establishing project roles, responsibilities & organization charts
B. Improving teamwork & project performance
C. Putting elements in place to manage conflicts & resolve issues
D. Producing a guide to team selection & assignment.

85. You are 4.5 months into a 6-month, $12,000 project with a planned linear spend. You have produced value of $8,500 and spent $10,000. What is your Estimate at Completion?

A. $13,500
B. $14,118
C. $2,118
D. $4,118.

86. You know that controlling scope is critical to your success as a project manager. What types of inputs would you want to have available to make you successful at this?

A. Verified deliverables
B. Approved change requests
C. Expert Judgment
D. Requirements traceability matrix.

87. The Cost Baseline for a project typically does not include:

A. Management reserves
B. Activity costs
C. Contingency reserves
D. Control accounts.

88. You are contemplating monitoring and control tools, and have heard that a Change Log can be useful. What is its purpose?

A. To address obstacles blocking the teams' performance
B. To document who is responsible for resolving issues that arise
C. To document and communicate both approved and rejected changes
D. To document and communicate approved changes.

89. In putting together your plan for performing Quality Assurance, in order to realize the key benefit, you must anticipate:

A. Facilitating the improvement of quality processes
B. Bringing objectivity to the customer acceptance process
C. Validating that work meets requirements
D. Allowing stakeholders to understand the current state of the project.

90. Often, a Multi-Criteria Decision Analysis is used to assist in making project staffing decisions. Some examples of selection criteria include:

A. Brainstorming Ability
B. Knowledge & Availability
C. Negotiation Skills
D. Sponsor Recommendation.

91. When closing a project or its procurements, you are:

A. Monitoring contract performance
B. Recording results of project quality activities
C. Measuring and analyzing project performance against the baseline
D. Releasing organization resources to new work and obtaining customer acceptance.

92. Your project currently has a schedule variance of -$100, and a cost variance of $200. The value that you have created thus far is $500. What is your SPI?

A. .83
B. -.83
C. 1.67
D. 600.

93. Managing stakeholder engagement involves activities such as:

A. Influencing stakeholders later in the project when their influence is highest
B. Using presentation, facilitation & listening techniques
C. Addressing potential stakeholder concerns and anticipating future problems
D. Employing information management systems and expert judgment.

94. A procurement statement of work would include:

A. Impacts to entities outside the performing organization
B. Guiding organizational principles
C. Quantity desired & work location
D. Project constraints and assumptions.

95. You have just created a document whose key benefit is a structured view of what has to be done. This is called:

A. A Project Plan
B. Project Requirements
C. A Project Scope Statement
D. A Work Breakdown Structure.

96. After completing your project's stakeholder analysis, you've identified a stakeholder who is highly interested in your project, but has little power to affect it. How should you manage that stakeholder?

A. Keep them satisfied
B. Manage them closely
C. Keep them informed
D. Monitor them occasionally.

97. Facilitation techniques used to guide development of the project charter include:

A. Nominal Group Technique
B. Brainstorming
C. Delphi Technique
D. Quality Function Deployment (QFD).

98. A communication method that is useful for a geographically distributed workforce due to the multiple project locations is:

A. Pull communication
B. Push communication
C. Interactive communication
D. Meetings.

99. When considering project roles & responsibilities, the following should be addressed:

A. Resource calendars & staff release plans
B. Responsibilities & competencies of the prospective team member
C. Recognition & reward criteria
D. Training needs.

100. ISO Quality Standards align with the *PMBOK® Guide,* and recognize the importance of:

A. Constrained Resources
B. Inspection over Prevention
C. Total Cost of Quality
D. Prevention Costs over Appraisal Costs.

101. What is the primary benefit of determining your budget?

A. It identifies the type of resources needed to complete the activity at hand
B. It provides the amount of time an activity will take to complete
C. It determines the cost required to complete project work
D. It determines the project's cost baseline.

102. What is the primary benefit of estimating activity resources?

A. It identifies the type of resources needed to complete the activity at hand
B. It provides the amount of time an activity will take to complete
C. It determines the cost required to complete project work
D. It determines the project's cost baseline.

103. Your project is currently focused on validating scope. What will you be bringing in to that activity, and what will you be creating?

A. You will bring in deliverables and create verified deliverables
B. You will bring in verified deliverables and create accepted deliverables
C. You will bring in verified deliverables and create validated deliverables
D. You will bring in change requests and create new deliverables.

104. In order to complete a project successfully, the team needs to:

A. Limit risk identification to key project subject matter experts
B. Use all of the processes in the *PMBOK® Guide*
C. Maintain communication and engagement with stakeholders
D. Share the stakeholder register with all stakeholders.

105. Progressive elaboration:

A. Has no place in managing a project, which is specific, unique and non-recurring
B. Is the process of dividing project scope into smaller, more manageable parts
C. Is synonymous with Agile methodology
D. Means that increasing detail is iterative as more information becomes available.

106. You are in the process of closing your project. Which of the following activities might you be addressing?

A. Claims administration
B. Early contract termination
C. Procurement audits & seller evaluations
D. Actions needed to collect project records.

107. A stakeholder classification model that categorizes stakeholders based on their power and legitimacy is a:

A. Power/Interest Grid
B. Salience Model
C. Power/Influence Grid
D. Influence/Impact Grid.

108. Organizational Process Assets Updates from the Close Procurements Process include deliverable acceptance documentation. This documentation requires:

A. Retention by the organization, if defined in the customer/provider agreement
B. Information on only conforming deliverables
C. Indexed contract documentation
D. A Requirements Traceability Matrix.

109. You are getting ready to identify your project risks. What tools or techniques are typically available to assist you?

A. Process analysis
B. Statistical sampling
C. Assumptions analysis & diagramming techniques
D. Meetings.

110. In addition to information in the register, the stakeholder management plan provides:

A. Roles and responsibilities
B. Reason for distribution of stakeholder information
C. Methods used to convey information
D. A glossary of common terminology.

111. You are project managing a team with a total size of 15 members, including you. A week ago, additional critical scope was added that will require you adding 5 members to your team to meet your date commitment, which will not be relaxed. How many communication channels are you adding to the team?

A. 90
B. 85
C. 105
D. 190.

112. Controlling schedules requires periodic performance review techniques that include:

A. Brainstorming
B. The Delphi Technique
C. Run Charts
D. Critical Chain Methodology.

113. You are operating in the Closing process group. What might you be doing?

A. Dealing with issues related to premature project closure
B. Recommending corrective actions
C. Completing the work defined in the project management plan
D. Dealing with trade-offs between budget and schedule activities.

114. The Conflict Management Style that would be least effective if the time constraint is severe and the positions are wide apart on the issue is:

A. Smoothing
B. Forcing
C. Collaborating
D. Compromising.

115. You are putting together your Cost Management Plan. In considering which organizational process assets might be helpful, you decide on:

A. Types of contracts to be used
B. Lessons learned & financial databases
C. Control thresholds & rules of performance measurement
D. Roles & responsibilities.

116. A Requirements Management Plan includes:

A. A process detailing how formal customer acceptance will be obtained
B. A process detailing how scope changes will be processed
C. Technology requirements
D. Products metrics to be used.

117. Meetings types include:

A. Information exchange or Decision making
B. Full Team or Partial Team
C. Stand-Up or Seated
D. Formal or Informal.

118. Project documents updated while planning risk responses include:

A. Outcomes of risks & their associated responses
B. Stakeholder tolerances & risk categories
C. Assumptions logs & change requests
D. Project schedule & stakeholder register.

119. Monitoring and Controlling Project Work:

A. Does not typically consume much of a project manager's time
B. Utilizes a Change Control Board (CCB)
C. Brings in project work performance data and outputs work performance information
D. Inputs project work performance information and outputs work performance reports.

120. A key benefit of validating scope is it:

A. Identifies causes of poor processes and validates work meets stakeholder requirements
B. Brings objectivity to the customer acceptance process
C. Releases organizational resources to pursue other enterprise work
D. Documents agreements for future reference.

121. You are talking to the contractor building your new home, who was very excited to find out that you are a project manager. You have asked him why there has been no noticeable activity on the site over the last week. He just informed you that a week ago, the foundation slab was poured, and that it must cure for ten days before framing activity can begin. This predecessor-successor relationship attribute is known as:

A. Lead
B. Mandatory
C. Lag
D. Fixed.

122. You are 4 months into a 6-month, $12,000 project with a planned linear spend. You have produced value of $8,000 and spent $9,000. Assuming you have corrected any issues causing your variances, what is your projected Variance at Completion?

A. $1,000
B. $0
C. $13,000
D. -$1,000.

123. In planning procurements, which of the following would likely be used as source selection criteria?

A. Cultural fit of the seller team
B. Life cycle costs and financial capacity
C. Gender balance of the bidder team
D. Pure project cost, without regard for life cycle costs past implementation.

124. A good project management plan (as opposed to project documents) includes:

A. A Change Management Plan
B. Project Calendars
C. Team Performance Assessments
D. A Stakeholder Register.

125. Your fellow PM has just stopped by your desk to chat. She sees that you are down in the dumps. When she asks why, you tell her that you're working a very labor intensive project, and struggling to organize the many types and number of resources. She suggests you use an RBS to categorize your resources hierarchically. An RBS, in this context, is a:

A. Risk Breakdown Structure
B. Resource Breakdown Structure
C. Resource Break-Fix
D. Responsibility Breakdown Structure.

126. A project was budgeted to take 2,000 hours of work. 750 hours have been burned, and 600 hours of value have actually been created. Your SPI is .9. What is the project's SV?

A. 150
B. -150
C. 67
D. -67.

127. The *PMBOK® Guide* contains:

A. 47 processes, 10 knowledge areas and 5 project groups
B. 42 processes, 10 knowledge areas and 5 process groups
C. 47 processes, 10 knowledge areas and 5 process groups
D. 42 processes, 9 knowledge areas and 5 process groups.

128. Conditions driving the business need for a project include:

A. Solution or quality requirements
B. Market demand or legal requirements
C. Transition or operational requirements
D. Training or quality requirements.

129. Group Decision-Making Techniques include:

A. Plurality
B. Consensus
C. Collaboration
D. Compromise.

130. At the beginning of your project, you and your sponsor agreed on acceptable limits for the project's process variables. You are now 3 months into the project. The sponsor is asking you if the variables are within those limits. To answer him, you consult your:

A. Run Chart
B. Control Chart
C. Scatter Diagram
D. Histogram.

131. A Quantitative Risk Analysis technique that uses simulations and probability distributions is:

A. Sensitivity analysis
B. Expected monetary value analysis
C. Monte Carlo technique
D. Expert Judgment.

132. Process group interactions mean that:

A. All process groups but Initiating & Closing overlap with each other over time
B. More project budget is spent in Planning than any other process group
C. All process groups overlap with each other over time
D. More project manager time is spent in Executing processes than elsewhere.

133. Configuration Management activities include which of the following?

A. Making a list of changes occurring during a project
B. Making a list of potential future project impacting events
C. Configuration status accounting
D. Configuration scope creep control.

134. Major components in a contract agreement would include:

A. Constraints & assumptions
B. Traceability objectives & business rules
C. Functional & non-functional requirements
D. Penalties & incentives.

135. You have been told that a project activity will most likely take 10 days. If all goes well, it will only take 6 days. However, if Murphy's law strikes, it could take 20 days. Given this uncertainty, you have decided to estimate the activity using a Beta, or PERT, distribution. You deliver an estimate of:

A. 10 days
B. 13 days
C. 12 Days
D. 11 Days.

136. A type of audit that identifies nonconforming organizational/project processes is a:

A. Procurement Audit
B. Quality Audit
C. Risk Audit
D. Tax Audit.

137. Arguably the most useful tool/technique used in qualifying risk, the Probability and Impact Matrix:

A. Is used in determining risk urgency levels
B. Marries probability and impact to rate risks as high, medium or low priority
C. Is used in categorizing risks
D. Is a statistical tool utilizing probability distributions.

138. You are exactly midway through a 6-month, $12,000 project with a planned linear spend. You have spent $4,000, and have produced value of $5,400. What is your CV?

A. -$1400
B. Not enough information to determine
C. 1.35
D. $1400.

139. Tools and Techniques used in the Close Project or Phase Process include:

A. Analytical techniques such as regression & trend analysis
B. Procurement negotiations
C. Records management systems
D. Procurement audits.

140. While working in the Planning processes, you will be:

A. Writing the project charter
B. Delineating the strategy and tactics for the project
C. Guiding project team selection and assignment
D. Reviewing change requests.

141. Organizational Process Assets Updates Outputs of the Close Project or Phase Process include which of the following?

A. Closed procurements
B. Final product, service or result transition
C. Project or phase closure documents
D. Procurement files.

142. You have just finished work on a document that includes a project scope statement, a WBS and a WBS dictionary. What have you just completed?

A. Performance Measurement Baseline
B. Requirements Document
C. SOW
D. Scope Baseline.

143. Dependency attributes include:

A. Mandatory or Discretionary
B. Fixed or Variable
C. Lead or Lag
D. PDM or ADM.

144. Work Performance Data

A. Are measurements integrated and analyzed in context
B. Are raw observations regarding such things as completion status of deliverables
C. Are physical representations of work performance
D. Are the same as Earned Value calculations.

145. When developing a project team, which tools might you use?

A. Networking & organizational theory
B. Negotiation & Multi-Criteria Decision Analysis
C. Team-Building activities & personnel assessment tools
D. Observation & Conversation.

146. You are considering bidding on a project that could be a real growth stimulator for your enterprise, but your limited capital resources just won't stretch to meet the requirements. You are considering entering into a joint venture with a larger company that you have partnered with in the past, and that has better capital resources at their disposal. What type of risk response strategy is this?

A. Mitigation
B. Transference
C. Sharing
D. Enhancement.

147. You are working on identifying project requirements. You decide to use a technique that enhances brainstorming with a voting process. You have chosen:

A. Idea/Mind Mapping
B. Nominal Group Technique
C. An Affinity Diagram
D. Multicriteria Decision Analysis.

148. You have decided to use the critical chain method to manage your project. Your concern is focused right now on managing three non-critical chains in your project network. You are considering:

A. Adding a project buffer to your network
B. Adding feeding buffers to the three non-critical chains
C. Managing the free float on your non-critical chains
D. Managing the total float on your non-critical chains.

149. Changes can be:

A. Corrective or Preventive
B. A planned workaround
C. Informal in nature
D. Approved by any project team member.

150. What should you tell a "reluctant sponsor" is the key benefit of developing a charter?

A. It defines the basis of all project work
B. It gets the project off to a good, formalized start
C. It describes the project, service or result boundaries for the project
D. It identifies the focus for groups of stakeholders.

Answers to *CAPM® Guide* 150-Question Sample Exam (3 Hour Time limit)

1. One key benefit of closing a project or phase is it:

A. Identifies causes of poor processes and validates work meets stakeholder requirements
B. Brings objectivity to the customer acceptance process
C. Releases organizational resources to pursue other enterprise work
D. Documents agreements for future reference.

Answer:

C. Releases organizational resources to pursue other enterprise work
PMBOK® Guide Reference: A.1.8.1
Process Group: Closing
Knowledge Area: Chapter 3; Integration

2. A project charter aligns the project with:

A. The project manager's work priorities
B. The strategy and ongoing work of the organization
C. The project's scope
D. The project management plan.

Answer:

B. The strategy and ongoing work of the organization
PMBOK® Guide Reference: 4.1
Process Group: Initiating
Knowledge Area: Integration

3. The key benefit of the Close Procurements Process is:

A. It increases the chance of final acceptance
B. It documents agreements for reference
C. It signals that all project activities are complete
D. It provides lessons learned.

Answer:

B. It documents agreements for reference
PMBOK® Guide Reference: 12.4
Process Group: Closing
Knowledge Area: Procurement

4. You are collecting requirements, and feel the need to be creative in your approach. To that end, what techniques could you employ with your team?

A. Regression analysis
B. Unanimity
C. Plurality
D. Affinity diagrams.

Answer:

D. Affinity diagrams
PMBOK® Guide Reference: 5.2.2.4
Process Group: Planning
Knowledge Area: Scope

5. Factors influencing make-buy decisions include

A. Associated risks
B. Clarity of vendor proposals
C. Outputs of a multi-criteria decision analysis
D. Level of vendor interest.

Answer:

A. Associated risks
PMBOK® Guide Reference: 12.2.1.6
Process Group: Executing
Knowledge Area: Procurement

6. You are concerned with the risk tolerance of a key stakeholder. What is risk tolerance?

A. Level of uncertainty at which that individual will have a specific interest
B. Degree of uncertainty that individual will take on in anticipation of a reward
C. Degree of risk that individual will withstand
D. The value that stakeholder assigns to a specific risk.

Answer:

C. Degree of risk that individual will withstand
PMBOK® Guide Reference: 11.0
Knowledge Area: Risk

7. You are in the midst of doing reserve analysis for your project. Your contingency reserves:

A. Are typically withheld for management control purposes
B. Are associated with the "known-unknowns" for your project
C. Are associated with the "unknown-unknowns" for your project
D. Are not included in the schedule baseline.

Answer:

B. Are associated with the "known-unknowns" for your project
PMBOK® Guide Reference: 6.5.2.6
Process Group: Planning
Knowledge Area: Time

8. Techniques for effective communications management include:

A. Nominal Group Technique
B. Observation and conversation
C. Delphi Technique
D. Choice of media and writing style.

Answer:

D. Choice of media and writing style
PMBOK® Guide Reference: 10.2
Process Group: Executing
Knowledge Area: Communication

9. Disadvantages of virtual teams include which of the following?

A. Exclusion of people with mobility issues
B. Exclusion of projects due to travel expense
C. Possibility of misunderstandings
D. Difficulty including geographically widespread staff.

Answer:

C. Possibility of misunderstandings
PMBOK® Guide Reference: 9.2.2.4
Process Group: Executing
Knowledge Area: Human Resource Management

10. You are exactly midway through a 6-month, $12,000 project with a planned linear spend. You have spent $8,000. What is your CPI?

A. -$2,000
B. Not enough information to determine
C. .75
D. 1.33.

Answer:

B. Not enough information to determine (You are given PV (half of the budget, or $6000) and AC ($8000); without EV, you cannot determine your CPI)
PMBOK® Guide Reference: 7.4, Table 7-1
Process Group: Monitoring & Controlling
Knowledge Area: Cost

11. The Monitoring & Controlling process group involves:

A. Influencing the factors that could circumvent integrated change control
B. Dealing with any premature project closure
C. Completing the work defined in the project management plan
D. Archiving relevant project documents.

Answer:

A. Influencing the factors that could circumvent integrated change control
PMBOK® Guide Reference: 3.6
Chapter 3

12. Your project sponsor has asked you to shave a week from your project schedule. There are no additional budget dollars to apply, so you decide to fast-track. This means you will likely:

A. Apply overtime
B. Overlap or parallel activities normally done in sequence
C. Accelerate non-critical path activities
D. Reduce scope.

Answer:

B. Overlap or parallel activities normally done in sequence
PMBOK® Guide Reference: 6.6.2.7
Process Group: Planning
Knowledge Area: Time

13. Objectives of developing a project team include:

A. Managing conflict constructively
B. Improving project member communications with key stakeholders
C. Improving feelings of trust
D. Selecting the appropriate power type to use in a situational context.

Answer:

C. Improving feelings of trust
PMBOK® Guide Reference: 9.3
Process Group: Executing
Knowledge Area: Human Resource Management

14. You have identified your stakeholders and produced your stakeholder management plan. Now you're proceeding to manage the engagement levels. Process inputs include:

A. Issue logs and work performance data
B. Issue logs and change requests
C. The project charter and project management plan
D. The communications management plan and change log.

Answer:

D. The communications management plan and change log
PMBOK® Guide Reference: 13.3.1
Process Group: Executing
Knowledge Area: Stakeholder Management

15. You are in the process of conducting procurements. What is the key benefit of this process?

A. Aligning internal & external stakeholder expectations
B. Determining the level and type of outside support needed for the project
C. Ensuring seller/buyer performance meet the requirements of the agreement
D. Providing the basis for defining and managing project & product scope.

Answer:

A. Aligning internal & external stakeholder expectations
PMBOK® Guide Reference: A.1.6.7
Process Group: Executing
Knowledge Area: Chapter 3; Procurement

16. Change requests:

A. Include workarounds
B. Can be formal or informal in nature
C. Include preventive actions and defect repairs
D. Often involve planning for workarounds.

Answer:

C. Include preventive actions and defect repairs
PMBOK® Guide Reference: 4.3.3.3
Process Group: Executing
Knowledge Area: Integration

17. You have learned that communications management involves considering the various dimensions of communication. They include:

A. Listening & questioning
B. Encoding & decoding
C. Push & pull
D. Verbal & non-verbal.

Answer:

D. Verbal & non-verbal
PMBOK® Guide Reference: 10.0
Knowledge Area: Communication

18. A colleague is confused about the difference between the project charter and scope statement. You tell him that the scope statement:

A. Contains high level requirements and risks
B. Addresses project exclusions, constraints and assumptions
C. Includes a list of key stakeholders
D. Contains project approval requirements, versus a charter's acceptance criteria.

Answer:

B. Addresses project exclusions, constraints and assumptions
PMBOK® Guide Reference: 5.3.3, Table 5-1
Process Group: Planning
Knowledge Area: Scope

19. Cause-and-effect diagrams are also known as:

A. Ishikawa diagrams
B. Pareto diagrams
C. Scatter diagrams
D. Histograms.

Answer:

A. Ishikawa diagrams
PMBOK® Guide Reference: 8.1.2.3
Process Group: Planning
Knowledge Area: Quality

20. You want to take a structured look at the effectiveness of your risk response strategies. You have therefore decided to:

A. Conduct a variance and trend analysis
B. Hold an all-team meeting to gather input
C. Do a risk reassessment
D. Conduct a risk audit.

Answer:

D. Conduct a risk audit
PMBOK® Guide Reference: 11.6.2.2
Process Group: Monitoring & Control
Knowledge Area: Risk

21. You have decided on a contract form for your project that allows for reimbursement of all legitimate seller costs, but pays a fee based solely on your subjective determination of seller performance. This contract form is:

A. Time and Materials
B. Cost Plus Award Fee
C. Cost Plus Incentive Fee
D. Cost Plus Fixed Fee.

Answer:

B. Cost Plus Award Fee
PMBOK® Guide Reference: 12.1.1.9
Process Group: Planning
Knowledge Area: Procurement

22. Estimate precision level is critical to understand before making commitments. You have determined your estimate to be in the -25% to +75% range. This is also known as a:

A. Definitive estimate
B. Budget estimate
C. Rough order of magnitude estimate
D. PERT estimate.

Answer:

C. Rough order of magnitude estimate
PMBOK® Guide Reference: 7.2
Process Group: Planning
Knowledge Area: Cost

23. The integrative nature of project management requires which process group to interact with the others?

A. Planning
B. Executing
C. Integrating
D. Monitoring & Controlling.

Answer:

D. Monitoring & Controlling
PMBOK® Guide Reference: 3.1, Figure 3-1
Process Group: Monitoring & Controlling; Chapter 3

24. In analyzing the engagement level of stakeholders, the current engagement levels are compared to desired levels to identify gaps and plans for closing them. Engagement levels for stakeholders include:

A. Unaware, Neutral & Leading
B. Expert, Referent and Legitimate
C. Withdrawing, Collaborating & Compromising
D. Resistant, Supportive & Coaching.

Answer:

A. Unaware, Neutral & Leading
PMBOK® Guide Reference: 13.2.2.3
Process Group: Planning
Knowledge Area: Stakeholder

25. Which of the following is true of a definitive estimate (also called grassroots, or engineering estimate):

A. It is generally accurate within plus or minus 10%
B. It is usually based on analogous information
C. It can be prepared quickly
D. It is also called a budget estimate.

Answer:

A. It is generally accurate within plus or minus 10%
PMBOK® Guide Reference: 6.5.2 (not specifically referenced, this estimate is the most detailed!)
Process Group: Planning
Knowledge Area: Time/Cost

26. Techniques for effective management of communications include:

A. Analysis of past performance
B. Push and pull communication
C. Project reports and lessons learned documentation
D. Choice of communications media and facilitation techniques.

Answer:

D. Choice of communications media and facilitation techniques
PMBOK® Guide Reference: 10.2
Process Group: Executing
Knowledge Area: Communication

27. A RACI Chart:

A. Is a form of an Organizational Breakdown Structure
B. Links the project team members to the work packages
C. Is an acronym that stands for Responsible, Analyze, Consult and Inquire
D. Is not particularly useful in a matrixed project organization structure.

Answer:

B. Links the project team members to the work packages
PMBOK® Guide Reference: 9.1.2.1
Process Group: Planning
Knowledge Area: Human Resource Management

28. Information gathering techniques used in identifying risks include:

A. Force field and multicriteria decision analysis
B. Idea/mind mapping and affinity diagrams
C. Interviewing & Root Cause Analysis
D. Cause-and-effect diagrams and flowcharts.

Answer:

C. Interviewing & Root Cause Analysis
PMBOK® Guide Reference: 11.2.2.2
Process Group: Planning
Knowledge Area: Risk

29. A Project Management Plan:

A. Is generally the same regardless of the complexity of a project
B. Is usually fairly static once put into motion
C. Should be consistent with the program management plan that drives it
D. Includes a section on maintenance of the product of the project.

Answer:

C. Should be consistent with the program management plan that drives it
PMBOK® Guide Reference: 4.2
Process Group: Planning
Knowledge Area: Integration

30. Solution requirements are grouped into:

A. Business & Stakeholder
B. Functional & Non-Functional
C. Quality & Scalability
D. Transition & Project.

Answer:

B. Functional & Non-Functional
PMBOK® Guide Reference: 5.2
Process Group: Planning
Knowledge Area: Scope

31. You are bidding on a project that is potentially very lucrative, but involves some new and highly unstable technology. You decide to proceed with the bid, but also price in some insurance with Lloyds of London in response to the risk level. What type of risk response strategy is this?

A. Mitigation
B. Transference
C. Sharing
D. Enhancement.

Answer:

B. Transference
PMBOK® Guide Reference: 11.5.2.1
Process Group: Planning
Knowledge Area: Risk

32. A Schedule Management Plan includes which of the following?

A. Rules of performance measurement & control thresholds
B. Process to control how change requests will be processed
C. Procedures for project cost reporting
D. A staffing management plan.

Answer:

A. Rules of performance measurement & control thresholds
PMBOK® Guide Reference: 6.1.3.1
Process Group: Planning
Knowledge Area: Time

33. You are working in the Initiating Process Group. During these processes:

A. The project management plan is developed
B. The strategy and tactics for the project are delineated
C. Project roles and responsibilities are established
D. Internal and External Stakeholders are identified.

Answer:

D. Internal and External Stakeholders are identified
PMBOK® Guide Reference: A.1.4
Process Group: Initiating
Chapter 3

34. You have just created a document which includes a set of deliverable acceptance criteria, project exclusions and assumptions & constraints. What is this document?

A. Project Plan
B. Project Requirements
C. Project Scope Statement
D. Work Breakdown Structure.

Answer:

C. Project Scope Statement
PMBOK® Guide Reference: 5.3.3.1
Process Group: Planning
Knowledge Area: Scope

35. You are planning for your project's procurements. You are likely:

A. Holding a Bidders Conference
B. Doing a Make-or-Buy Analysis
C. Advertising
D. Getting Independent Estimates.

Answer:

B. Doing a Make-or-Buy Analysis
PMBOK® Guide Reference: 12.1.2.1
Process Group: Planning
Knowledge Area: Procurement

36. Communication Models are important for a project manager to understand in planning communication for their project. As part of the basic communication model:

A. The receiver of the information is responsible for understanding and acknowledging it
B. The receiver of the information is responsible for responding and agreeing to it
C. The complete sequence of model steps is to Transmit, Decode and provide Feedback
D. Noise is not typically an issue.

Answer:

A. The receiver of the information is responsible for understanding and acknowledging it
PMBOK® Guide Reference: 10.1.2.3
Process Group: Planning
Knowledge Area: Communication

37. You are in the process of monitoring your project. This involves:

A. Increasing stakeholder support and minimizing resistance
B. Managing communications
C. Measuring and analyzing project performance against the baseline
D. Coordinating the people & resources performing the work.

C. Measuring and analyzing project performance against the baseline
PMBOK® Guide Reference: A.1.7
Process Group: Monitoring & Controlling
Chapter 3

38. The most common type of dependency relationship found in the Precedence Diagramming Method (PDM), which requires completion of a predecessor before a successor can begin, is called:

A. Finish-To-Finish
B. Start-To-Finish
C. Finish-To-Start
D. Start-To-Start.

Answer:

C. Finish-To-Start
PMBOK® Guide Reference: 6.3.2.1
Process Group: Planning
Knowledge Area: Time

39. The term that takes in all prevention/appraisal costs over the life of the product is:

A. Cost of Quality
B. Cost-Benefit Analysis
C. Cost of Non-Conformance
D. Cost of Conformance.

Answer:

A. Cost of Quality
PMBOK® Guide Reference: 8.1.2.2
Process Group: Planning
Knowledge Area: Quality

40. A Scope Management Plan includes:

A. Business requirements
B. A process which enables creation of a WBS
C. Quality requirements
D. Training requirements.

Answer:

B. A process which enables creation of a WBS
PMBOK® Guide Reference: 5.1.3.1
Process Group: Planning
Knowledge Area: Scope

41. Inputs used in determining your project budget include:

A. Run Charts & Control Charts
B. Reserve Analysis & Cost Aggregation
C. Risk Register & Basis of Estimates
D. Work Performance Data & Project Funding Requirements.

Answer:

C. Risk Register & Basis of Estimates
PMBOK® Guide Reference: 12.2.2.1
Process Group: Executing
Knowledge Area: Procurement

42. In conducting procurements, a tool used to bring the buyer and potential sellers together prior to proposal submittals is a(n):

A. Proposal pre-evaluation
B. Independent estimate gathering
C. Procurement negotiation
D. Bidder conference.

Answer:

D. Bidder conference
PMBOK® Guide Reference: 12.2.2.1
Process Group: Executing
Knowledge Area: Procurement

43. You have just finished your probability & impact assessment and risk categorization. You have a long list of risks. What should you do next?

A. A risk urgency assessment
B. Qualitative risk analysis
C. Quantitative risk analysis
D. Risk response planning.

Answer:

A. A risk urgency assessment
PMBOK® Guide Reference: 11.3.2.5
Process Group: Planning
Knowledge Area: Risk

44. You are debating the benefit of Integrated Change Control with a colleague. He says it's minimizing baseline changes. You think it's:

A. Allowing stakeholders to understand the current project state
B. Ensuring an optimal information flow
C. Allowing for changes to be considered in an integrated manner while reducing risk
D. Providing overall management of project work.

Answer:

C. Allowing for changes to be considered in an integrated manner while reducing risk
PMBOK® Guide Reference: 4.5
Process Group: Monitoring & Controlling
Knowledge Area: Integration

45. Project Management Processes:

A. Ensure the effective life cycle flow of the project
B. Create the project's product
C. Vary by application area
D. Specify the project's product.

Answer:

A. Ensure the effective life cycle flow of the project
PMBOK® Guide Reference: 3.0, P 47
Chapter 3

46. You are considering techniques to control stakeholder engagement. You choose from:

A. Communication methods, interpersonal skills & management skills
B. Information management systems, expert judgment and meetings
C. Analytical techniques, expert judgment and meetings
D. Stakeholder analysis, expert judgment and meetings.

Answer:

B. Information management systems, expert judgment and meetings
PMBOK® Guide Reference: 13.4.2
Process Group: Monitoring & Controlling
Knowledge Area: Stakeholder Management

47. You have a risk that doesn't lend itself to a suitable response strategy. You have decided to establish a budget reserve should it occur. What response strategy is this?

A. Mitigation
B. Passive acceptance
C. Active acceptance
D. Avoidance.

Answer:

C. Active acceptance
PMBOK® Guide Reference: 11.5.2.1
Process Group: Planning
Knowledge Area: Risk

48. Assuming that your team is one that has begun to work together well, has developed a trusting relationship, but has not yet reached its peak output, what stage of development have they reached?

A. Forming
B. Storming
C. Performing
D. Norming.

Answer:

D. Norming
PMBOK® Guide Reference: 9.3.2.3
Process Group: Executing
Knowledge Area: Human Resource Management

49. Quality Management and Control tools unique to assurance activities include:

A. Matrix Diagrams & Prioritization Matrices
B. Cause & Effect Diagrams
C. Pareto Diagrams
D. Control Charts.

Answer:

A. Matrix Diagrams & Prioritization Matrices
PMBOK® Guide Reference: 8.2.2.1
Process Group: Executing
Knowledge Area: Quality

Use the following data for the next two questions:

You have the following set of six project activities, with associated task durations and predecessor/successor relationships.

A: 2 days; no predecessors
B: 3 days; no predecessors
C: 4 days; both A & B are predecessors
D: 3 days; A is a predecessor
E: 2 days; B is a predecessor
F: 1 day; both C & E are predecessors

50. What is your critical path, and its length?

A. ACF; 7 Days
B. BCF; 8 Days
C. BEF; 8 Days
D. None of the above.

Answer:

B. BCF; 8 Days

Time Management Network Diagram

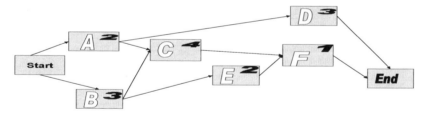

PMBOK® Guide Reference: 6.6.2.2
Process Group: Planning
Knowledge Area: Time

51. More content has been added to Task F, extending its duration to 2 days, and your critical path by one day. To make things worse, your boss has told you that the work must be completed in 6 days, at the lowest possible cost. Looking at the table below, which tasks would you crash, in what sequence, and what would your crashing cost be?

Task	Schedule Days	Crashable Days	Crash Cost/Day
A	2	1	1000
B	3	1	4000
C	4	2	10000
D	3	2	1000
E	2	1	1000
F	2	1	2000

A. D, E & F; $4,000
B. F, E & B; $7,000
C. F, A & C: $13,000
D. F, B & C; $16,000.

Answer:

D. F, B & C; $16,000.

Crashing F first costs $2,000, and shortens two paths currently above 6 days, leaving only ACF (7) and BCF (8) above 6 days. F is now fully crashed, leaving only A, B & C as potential crashable tasks.

Crashing B next costs $4,000, and shortens BCF to 7 days. B is now also fully crashed.

Crashing C next meets the objective of 6 days for the schedule, shortening both ACF and BCF to 6 days at a cost of $10,000. Total cost of crashing is $2K+$4K+$10K, or $16,000.

Note that Task A, which appeared to be a low cost candidate to crash, did not come into play, as the necessity of crashing C and F to reduce critical path BCF by three days also reduced path ACF to 6 days.

PMBOK® Guide Reference: 6.6.2.7
Process Group: Planning
Knowledge Area: Time

52. You are in the process of identifying project risks. Why should you do this?

A. It ensures that risk management is commensurate with the project's importance
B. It enables project managers to focus on high-priority risks
C. It provides the project team the ability to anticipate events
D. It allows the project manager to focus on the right groups of stakeholders.

Answer:

C. It provides the project team the ability to anticipate events
PMBOK® Guide Reference: A.1.5.19
Process Group: Planning
Knowledge Area: Chapter 3; Risk

53. Appendix X3 was added in *PMBOK® Guide* Ed 4, to highlight the importance of a project manager's soft skills. Which of the following skills are on the Appendix X3 list?

A. Trust Building, Conflict Management & Coaching
B. Power, Leadership and Cultural Awareness
C. Facilitation, Motivation & Communication
D. Meeting Management, Decision Making & Negotiation.

Answer:

A. Trust Building, Conflict Management & Coaching
PMBOK® Guide Reference: Appendix X3
Process Group: Executing
Knowledge Area: Human Resource Management

54. You have been considering going beyond the simple status report and doing some more elaborate performance reporting for your project. What might you produce?

A. Percent complete report
B. Progress measurements
C. Status dashboards
D. Analysis of past performance.

Answer:

D. Analysis of past performance
PMBOK® Guide Reference: 10.2.2.5
Process Group: Executing
Knowledge Area: Communication

55. Effective cost control requires:

A. Conducting retrospective reviews & reprioritizing the work backlog
B. Reserve Analysis & Cost Aggregation
C. Influencing change factors and managing them as they occur
D. Ensuring that project outputs meet the requirements.

Answer:

C. Influencing change factors and managing them as they occur
PMBOK® Guide Reference: 7.4
Process Group: Monitoring & Controlling
Knowledge Area: Cost

56. Inputs that may be of particular use to you in controlling your procurements include:

A. Agreements and approved change requests
B. Issue logs
C. Project funding requirements
D. Project schedule.

Answer:

A. Agreements and approved change requests
PMBOK® Guide Reference: 12.3.1
Process Group: Monitoring & Controlling
Knowledge Area: Procurement

57. The Qualitative Risk Analysis key benefit is:

A. It ensures that risk management is commensurate with the project's importance
B. It enables project managers to focus on high-priority risks
C. It provides the project team the ability to anticipate events
D. It produces quantitative risk information to support decision making.

Answer:

B. It enables project managers to focus on high-priority risks
PMBOK® Guide Reference: 11.3
Process Group: Planning
Knowledge Area: Risk

58. A resource breakdown structure (RBS):

A. Is a hierarchical list of resources by category
B. Breaks the project's deliverables into work packages
C. Is a hierarchical list of risks organized by categories
D. Shows the project's work organized by work departments.

Answer:

A. Is a hierarchical list of resources by category
PMBOK® Guide Reference: 9.1.2.1
Process Group: Planning
Knowledge Area: Human Resource Management

59. The project charter accomplishes which of the following?

A. Defines how the project is to be executed, monitored, controlled & closed
B. Establishes the project manager's ownership, as its sponsor
C. Authorizes the sponsor to run the project
D. Enables partnering of the performing and requesting organizations.

Answer:

D. Enables partnering of the performing and requesting organizations
PMBOK® Guide Reference: 4.1
Process Group: Initiating
Knowledge Area: Integration

60. The five Process Groups are:

A. Closing, Executing, Monitoring, Controlling, and Initiating
B. Planning, Closing, Monitoring & Controlling, Managing and Initiating
C. Planning, Closing, Executing, Monitoring & Controlling, and Initiating
D Executing, Monitoring, Controlling, Planning and Initiating.

Answer:

C. Planning, Closing, Executing, Monitoring & Controlling, and Initiating
PMBOK Reference: Table 3-1, P 61
Chapter 3

61. Enterprise Environmental factors affecting the sequencing of a project's schedule activities include:

A. Planning policies, procedures & guidelines
B. Company work authorization systems
C. Schedule network templates
D. Project files from the corporate knowledge base.

Answer:

B. Company work authorization systems
PMBOK® Guide Reference: 6.3.1.6
Process Group: Planning
Knowledge Area: Time

62. A Requirements Management Plan includes:

A. Product metrics and a rationale for their use
B. A process that enables creation of a WBS
C. Support and training requirements
D. Acceptance criteria.

Answer:

A. Product metrics and a rationale for their use
PMBOK® Guide Reference: 5.1.3.2
Process Group: Planning
Knowledge Area: Scope

63. The stakeholder management plan is:

A. Most effective when widely distributed for comment
B. A document whose key benefit is identifying a stakeholder communication approach
C. A document containing all relevant stakeholder details
D. A sensitive document whose distribution should be limited.

Answer:

D. A sensitive document whose distribution should be limited
PMBOK® Guide Reference: 13.2.3.1
Process Group: Planning
Knowledge Area: Stakeholder Management

64. Which of the following is true about statistical control processes?

A. Attribute sampling determines whether a result conforms or not
B. Variables sampling defines a range of acceptable results
C. Tolerances identify boundaries of common statistical variation
D. Control limits measure the result on a continuous scale of conformity.

Answer:

A. Attribute sampling determines whether a result conforms or not
PMBOK® Guide Reference: 8.3
Process Group: Monitoring & Control
Knowledge Area: Quality

65. You have just finished your risk management plan. What did it likely include?

A. Response strategies & contingency plans
B. Roles & responsibilities, risk process timing & risk categories
C. A list of risks & potential responses
D. A probability of achieving cost & time objectives.

Answer:

B. Roles & responsibilities, risk process timing & risk categories
PMBOK® Guide Reference: 11.1.3.1
Process Group: Planning
Knowledge Area: Risk

66. A good cost management plan includes:

A. A project organization chart
B. Types of contracts to be used and any potential risk management issues
C. Control thresholds & rules of performance measurement
D. A process specifying how product acceptance will be obtained.

Answer:

C. Control thresholds & rules of performance measurement
PMBOK® Guide Reference: 7.1.3.1
Process Group: Planning
Knowledge Area: Cost

67. You are in the process of executing the project's work. You are:

A. Formally completing the project
B. Planning responses to risk events
C. Measuring and analyzing project performance
D. Coordinating people & resources.

D. Coordinating people & resources
PMBOK® Guide Reference: A.1.6
Process Group: Executing
Chapter 3

68. A Requirements Traceability Matrix traces requirements for which of the following?

A. Test strategy & scenarios
B. Production support
C. Product scope
D. The WBS.

Answer:

A. Test strategy & scenarios
PMBOK® Guide Reference: 5.2.3.2
Process Group: Planning
Knowledge Area: Scope

69. Information considerations to take into account when working in the communications management knowledge area include:

A. Encoding & decoding mechanisms
B. Escalation processes
C. Storage format and manner of retrieval
D. Meeting management techniques.

Answer:

C. Storage format and manner of retrieval
PMBOK® Guide Reference: 10.0
Knowledge Area: Communication

70. Scope verification & quality control:

A. Are the same
B. Differ, in that scope verification is concerned with deliverables acceptance, and quality control with the correctness of those deliverables
C. Usually happen simultaneously
D. Differ, in that quality control is concerned with deliverables acceptance, and scope validation with the correctness of those deliverables.

Answer:

B. Differ, in that scope validation is concerned with deliverables acceptance, and quality control with the correctness of those deliverables
PMBOK® Guide Reference: 5.5
Process Group: Monitoring & Controlling
Knowledge Area: Scope

71. The Project Management Information System (PMIS):

A. Is the part of organizational process assets providing access to tools
B. Does not include automated gathering methods
C. Is a component of the project management plan
D. Is the part of enterprise environmental factors providing access to tools.

Answer:

D. Is the part of enterprise environmental factors providing access to tools
PMBOK® Guide Reference: 4.3.2.2
Process Group: Executing
Knowledge Area: Integration

72. You have just finished your Staffing Management Plan. What did it include?

A. Resource calendars & staff release plans
B. A list of project roles & responsibilities
C. Competencies needed to accomplish the project's work
D. A glossary of common project terminology.

Answer:

A. Resource calendars & staff release plans
PMBOK® Guide Reference: 9.1.3.1
Process Group: Planning
Knowledge Area: Human Resource Management

73. The key benefit of identifying stakeholders is:

A. Finding out who your stakeholders really are
B. Its impact on keeping scope under control
C. Identifying the right focus for each stakeholder group
D. Its impact on the communication plan.

Answer:

C. Identifying the right focus for each stakeholder group
PMBOK Reference: 13.1
Process Group: Initiating
Knowledge Area: Stakeholder

74. In addition to the seven basic quality management tools and quality management and control tools, an additional quality tool for diagramming pro-anti change degree is the:

A. Pareto diagram
B. Force field analysis
C. Nominal group technique
D. Flowchart.

Answer:

B. Force field analysis
PMBOK® Guide Reference: 8.1.2.7
Process Group: Planning
Knowledge Area: Quality

75. Knowledge Areas include:

A. Scope, Time, Cost & Procurement
B. Quality, Risk, Communication and Planning
C. Integration, Initiating, Stakeholder and Human Resources
D. Scope, Time, Cost & Closing.

Answer:

A. Scope, Time, Cost & Procurement
PMBOK Reference: Table 3-1, P 61
Chapter 3

76. Early contract termination:

A. Does not require compensation for any work related to the terminated contract part
B. If invoked, gives the buyer termination rights only on the entire contract
C. Results from successful completion of the project
D. Can result from mutual agreement or default of one of the parties.

Answer:

D. Can result from mutual agreement or default of one of the parties
PMBOK® Guide Reference: 12.4
Process Group: Closing
Knowledge Area: Procurement

77. You are trying to decide whether to build or outsource a solution component for a new product expected to generate $300,000 in sales over its life cycle. If you build, it will cost $50,000. If you outsource, it will cost $45,000. You estimate a 5% chance of experiencing customer returns if you build, and 20% if you outsource. Those customer returns would cost you $20,000. Absent of other decision criteria, what is your decision?

A. Build, because $65,000 in estimated costs is less than $70,000
B. Outsource, because $49,000 in estimated costs is less than $51,000
C. Build, because $49,000 in estimated costs is less than $51,000
D. Outsource, because $65,000 in estimated costs is less than $70,000.

Answer:

B. Outsource: $49K in est. costs is less than $51K (In this decision tree, building costs $51K ($50K plus 5% times $20K) and buying costs $49K ($45K plus 20% times $20K)
PMBOK® Guide Reference: 11.4.2.2
Process Group: Planning
Knowledge Area: Risk

78. What is the key purpose for controlling project communication?

A. To effectively engage stakeholders
B. To document the project's approach to ensure efficient communications
C. To ensure optimal communication flow
D. To minimize stakeholder resistance & increase support.

Answer:

C. To ensure optimal communication flow
PMBOK Reference: 10.3
Process Group: Monitoring & Controlling
Knowledge Area: Communication

79. You were just in a meeting and heard someone mention something called the "100 percent rule". Immediately after the meeting you pulled up Wikipedia to find out what the term refers to. You found that it means:

A. A Decision Tree accounts for 100% of its event probabilities
B. The work at any WBS level should roll up to higher levels so that nothing is omitted
C. BAC equals 100% of the work to be performed, or 100% of the PVs
D. All of the communication channels on a project need to be accounted for in planning.

Answer:

B. The work at any WBS level should roll up to higher levels so that nothing is omitted
PMBOK® Guide Reference: 5.4.2
Process Group: Planning
Knowledge Area: Scope

80. The Perform Integrated Change Control Process:

A. Begins sometime after the project's inception
B. Accepts changes in both oral and written form
C. Often employs a Change Control Board to review/evaluate changes
D. Requires only the approval of the project manager to move changes forward.

Answer:

C. Often employs a Change Control Board to review/evaluate changes
PMBOK® Guide Reference: 4.5
Process Group: Monitoring & Control
Knowledge Area: Integration

81. You are at the point in your project where you have to begin controlling stakeholder engagement. You are looking through your project plan for information such as:

A. The change management plan, and how human resource requirements will be met
B. Historical information about previous similar projects
C. A description of the organizational culture & political climate
D. Schedules and statements of work.

Answer:

A. The change management plan, and how human resource requirements will be met
PMBOK® Guide Reference: 13.4.1.1
Process Group: Monitoring & Controlling
Knowledge Area: Stakeholder Management

82. You are working on a project that is projected to take 12 months to complete. The first three months of activity are very well-defined at this point, but the rest of the work schedule looks very hazy to you. What activity definition technique might you use to your advantage in this situation?

A. Joint Application Design
B. Progressive Elaboration
C. Rolling Wave Planning
D. Decomposition.

Answer:

C. Rolling Wave Planning
PMBOK® Guide Reference: 6.2.2.2
Process Group: Planning
Knowledge Area: Time

83. Process groups

A. Will never be conducted within a single phase
B. Are equivalent to project life cycle phases
C. Are typically not reused during the project life cycle
D. Are not project life cycle phases.

Answer:

D. Are not project life cycle phases
PMBOK® Guide Reference: 3.2, P 52
Chapter 3

84. In using a process to acquire your project team, the key benefit to you is:

A. Establishing project roles, responsibilities & organization charts
B. Improving teamwork & project performance
C. Putting elements in place to manage conflicts & resolve issues
D. Producing a guide to team selection & assignment.

Answer:

D. Producing a guide to team selection & assignment
PMBOK® Guide Reference: 9.2
Process Group: Executing
Knowledge Area: Human Resource Management

85. You are 4.5 months into a 6-month, $12,000 project with a planned linear spend. You have produced value of $8,500 and spent $10,000. What is your Estimate at Completion?

A. $13,500
B. $14,118
C. $2,118
D. $4,118.

Answer:

B. $14,118 (Equation assumption for EAC = BAC/CPI; CPI = EV/AC = $8500/$10000 = .85; EAC = $12000/.85 = $14,118)
PMBOK® Guide Reference: 7.4, Table 7-1
Process Group: Monitoring & Controlling
Knowledge Area: Cost

86. You know that controlling scope is critical to your success as a project manager. What types of inputs would you want to have available to make you successful at this?

A. Verified deliverables
B. Approved change requests
C. Expert Judgment
D. Requirements traceability matrix.

Answer:

D. Requirements traceability matrix
PMBOK® Guide Reference: 5.6.1.3
Process Group: Monitoring & Controlling
Knowledge Area: Scope

87. The Cost Baseline for a project typically does not include:

A. Management reserves
B. Activity costs
C. Contingency reserves
D. Control accounts.

Answer:

A. Management reserves
PMBOK® Guide Reference: 7.3.3.1 (Figure 7-8)
Process Group: Planning
Knowledge Area: Cost

88. You are contemplating monitoring and control tools, and have heard that a Change Log can be useful. What is its purpose?

A. To address obstacles blocking the teams' performance
B. To document who is responsible for resolving issues that arise
C. To document and communicate both approved and rejected changes
D. To document and communicate approved changes.

Answer:

C. To document and communicate both approved and rejected changes
PMBOK® Guide Reference: 4.5.3.2
Process Group: Monitoring & Controlling
Knowledge Area: Integration

89. In putting together your plan for performing Quality Assurance, in order to realize the key benefit, you must anticipate:

A. Facilitating the improvement of quality processes
B. Bringing objectivity to the customer acceptance process
C. Validating that work meets requirements
D. Allowing stakeholders to understand the current state of the project.

Answer:

A. Facilitating the improvement of quality processes
PMBOK® Guide Reference: 8.2
Process Group: Executing
Knowledge Area: Quality

90. Often, a Multi-Criteria Decision Analysis is used to assist in making project staffing decisions. Some examples of selection criteria include:

A. Brainstorming Ability
B. Knowledge & Availability
C. Negotiation Skills
D. Sponsor Recommendation.

Answer:

B. Knowledge & Availability
PMBOK® Guide Reference: 9.2.2.5
Process Group: Executing
Knowledge Area: Human Resource Management

91. When closing a project or its procurements, you are:

A. Monitoring contract performance
B. Recording results of project quality activities
C. Measuring and analyzing project performance against the baseline
D. Releasing organization resources to new work and obtaining customer acceptance.

Answer:

D. Releasing organization resources to new work and obtaining customer acceptance
PMBOK® Guide Reference: A.1.8.1
Process Group: Closing
Chapter 3

92. Your project currently has a schedule variance of -$100, and a cost variance of $200. The value that you have created thus far is $500. What is your SPI?

A. .83
B. -.83
C. 1.67
D. 600.

Answer: A. .83 (SV = -$100; PV = EV–SV = $600; SPI = EV/SV = 500/600 = .83)
PMBOK® Guide Reference: 6.7.2.1
Process Group: Monitoring & Controlling
Knowledge Area: Time

93. Managing stakeholder engagement involves activities such as:

A. Influencing stakeholders later in the project when their influence is highest
B. Using presentation, facilitation & listening techniques
C. Addressing potential stakeholder concerns and anticipating future problems
D. Employing information management systems and expert judgment.

Answer:

C. Addressing potential stakeholder concerns and anticipating future problems
PMBOK® Guide Reference: 13.3
Process Group: Executing
Knowledge Area: Stakeholder Management

94. A procurement statement of work would include:

A. Impacts to entities outside the performing organization
B. Guiding organizational principles
C. Quantity desired & work location
D. Project constraints and assumptions.

Answer:
C. Quantity desired & work location
PMBOK® Guide Reference: 12.2.1.7
Process Group: Executing
Knowledge Area: Procurement

95. You have just created a document whose key benefit is a structured view of what has to be done. This is called:

A. A Project Plan
B. Project Requirements
C. A Project Scope Statement
D. A Work Breakdown Structure.

Answer:

D. A Work Breakdown Structure
PMBOK® Guide Reference: 5.4
Process Group: Planning
Knowledge Area: Scope

96. After completing your project's stakeholder analysis, you've identified a stakeholder who is highly interested in your project, but has little power to affect it. How should you manage that stakeholder?

A. Keep them satisfied
B. Manage them closely
C. Keep them informed
D. Monitor them occasionally.

Answer:

C. Keep them informed
PMBOK® Guide Reference: 13.1.2.1
Process Group: Initiating
Knowledge Area: Stakeholder

97. Facilitation techniques used to guide development of the project charter include:

A. Nominal Group Technique
B. Brainstorming
C. Delphi Technique
D. Quality Function Deployment (QFD).

Answer:

B. Brainstorming
PMBOK® Guide Reference: 4.1.2.2
Process Group: Initiating
Knowledge Area: Integration

98. A communication method that is useful for a geographically distributed workforce due to the multiple project locations is:

A. Pull communication
B. Push communication
C. Interactive communication
D. Meetings.

Answer:

A. Pull communication
PMBOK® Guide Reference: 10.1.2.4
Process Group: Planning
Knowledge Area: Communications

99. When considering project roles & responsibilities, the following should be addressed:

A. Resource calendars & staff release plans
B. Responsibilities & competencies of the prospective team member
C. Recognition & reward criteria
D. Training needs.

Answer:

B. Responsibilities & competencies of the prospective team member
PMBOK® Guide Reference: 9.1.3.1
Process Group: Planning
Knowledge Area: Human Resource Management

100. ISO Quality Standards align with the *PMBOK® Guide,* and recognize the importance of:

A. Constrained Resources
B. Inspection over Prevention
C. Total Cost of Quality
D. Prevention Costs over Appraisal Costs.

Answer:

C. Total Cost of Quality
PMBOK® Guide Reference: 8.0, P 229
Knowledge Area: Quality

101. What is the primary benefit of determining your budget?

A. It identifies the type of resources needed to complete the activity at hand
B. It provides the amount of time an activity will take to complete
C. It determines the cost required to complete project work
D. It determines the project's cost baseline.

Answer:

D. It determines the project's cost baseline
PMBOK® Guide Reference: 7.3
Process Group: Planning
Knowledge Area: Cost

102. What is the primary benefit of estimating activity resources?

A. It identifies the type of resources needed to complete the activity at hand
B. It provides the amount of time an activity will take to complete
C. It determines the cost required to complete project work
D. It determines the project's cost baseline.

Answer:

A. It identifies the type of resources needed to complete the activity at hand
PMBOK® Guide Reference: 6.4
Process Group: Planning
Knowledge Area: Time

103. Your project is currently focused on validating scope. What will you be bringing in to that activity, and what will you be creating?

A. You will bring in deliverables and create verified deliverables
B. You will bring in verified deliverables and create accepted deliverables
C. You will bring in verified deliverables and create validated deliverables
D. You will bring in change requests and create new deliverables.

Answer:

B. You will bring in verified deliverables and create accepted deliverables
PMBOK® Guide Reference: 5.5.1, 5.5.3
Process Group: Monitoring & Controlling
Knowledge Area: Scope

104. In order to complete a project successfully, the team needs to:

A. Limit risk identification to key project subject matter experts
B. Use all of the processes in the *PMBOK® Guide*
C. Maintain communication and engagement with stakeholders
D. Share the stakeholder register with all stakeholders.

Answer:

C. Maintain communication and engagement with stakeholders
PMBOK® Guide Reference: 3.0, P 47
Chapter 3

105. Progressive elaboration:

A. Has no place in managing a project, which is specific, unique and non-recurring
B. Is the process of dividing project scope into smaller, more manageable parts
C. Is synonymous with Agile methodology
D. Means that increasing detail is iterative as more information becomes available.

Answer:

D. Means that increasing detail is iterative as more information becomes available
PMBOK® Guide Reference: 3.4, P 55; Glossary
Chapter 3

106. You are in the process of closing your project. Which of the following activities might you be addressing?

A. Claims administration
B. Early contract termination
C. Procurement audits & seller evaluations
D. Actions needed to collect project records.

Answer:

D. Actions needed to collect project records
PMBOK® Guide Reference: 4.6
Process Group: Closing
Knowledge Area: Integration

107. A stakeholder classification model that categorizes stakeholders based on their power and legitimacy is a:

A. Power/Interest Grid
B. Salience Model
C. Power/Influence Grid
D. Influence/Impact Grid.

Answer:

B. Salience Model
PMBOK® Guide Reference: 13.1.2.1
Process Group: Initiating
Knowledge Area: Stakeholder

108. Organizational Process Assets Updates from the Close Procurements Process include deliverable acceptance documentation. This documentation requires:

A. Retention by the organization, if defined in the customer/provider agreement
B. Information on only conforming deliverables
C. Indexed contract documentation
D. A Requirements Traceability Matrix.

Answer:

A. Retention by the organization, if defined in the customer/provider agreement
PMBOK® Guide Reference: 12.4.3.2
Process Group: Closing
Knowledge Area: Procurement

109. You are getting ready to identify your project risks. What tools or techniques are typically available to assist you?

A. Process analysis
B. Statistical sampling
C. Assumptions analysis & diagramming techniques
D. Meetings.

Answer:

C. Assumptions analysis & diagramming techniques
PMBOK® Guide Reference: 11.2.2
Process Group: Planning
Knowledge Area: Risk

110. In addition to information in the register, the stakeholder management plan provides:

A. Roles and responsibilities
B. Reason for distribution of stakeholder information
C. Methods used to convey information
D. A glossary of common terminology.

Answer:

B. Reason for distribution of stakeholder information
PMBOK® Guide Reference: 13.2.3.1
Process Group: Planning
Knowledge Area: Stakeholder

111. You are project managing a team with a total size of 15 members, including you. A week ago, additional critical scope was added that will require you adding 5 members to your team to meet your date commitment, which will not be relaxed. How many communication channels are you adding to the team?

A. 90
B. 85
C. 105
D. 190.

Answer:

B. 85; Channels presently equal (15(15-1))/2, or 105. Adding 5 members to the team moves that number to ((20(20-1))/2, or 190. 190 minus 105 equals 85.
PMBOK® Guide Reference: 10.1.2.1
Process Group: Planning
Knowledge Area: Communication

112. Controlling schedules requires periodic performance review techniques that include:

A. Brainstorming
B. The Delphi Technique
C. Run Charts
D. Critical Chain Methodology.

Answer:

D. Critical chain methodology
PMBOK® Guide Reference: 6.7.2.1
Process Group: Monitoring & Control
Knowledge Area: Time

113. You are operating in the Closing process group. What might you be doing?

A. Dealing with issues related to premature project closure
B. Recommending corrective actions
C. Completing the work defined in the project management plan
D. Dealing with trade-offs between budget and schedule activities.

Answer:

A. Dealing with issues related to premature project closure
PMBOK® Guide Reference: 3.7
Chapter 3

114. The Conflict Management Style that would be least effective if the time constraint is severe and the positions are wide apart on the issue is:

A. Smoothing
B. Forcing
C. Collaborating
D. Compromising.

Answer:

C. Collaborating
PMBOK® Guide Reference: 9.4.2.3
Process Group: Executing
Knowledge Area: Human Resource Management

115. You are putting together your Cost Management Plan. In considering which organizational process assets might be helpful, you decide on:

A. Types of contracts to be used
B. Lessons learned & financial databases
C. Control thresholds & rules of performance measurement
D. Roles & responsibilities.

Answer:

B. Lessons learned & financial databases
PMBOK® Guide Reference: 7.1.1.4
Process Group: Planning
Knowledge Area: Cost

116. A Requirements Management Plan includes:

A. A process detailing how formal customer acceptance will be obtained
B. A process detailing how scope changes will be processed
C. Technology requirements
D. Products metrics to be used.

Answer:

D. Products metrics to be used
PMBOK® Guide Reference: 5.1.3.2
Process Group: Planning
Knowledge Area: Scope

117. Meetings types include:

A. Information exchange or Decision making
B. Full Team or Partial Team
C. Stand-Up or Seated
D. Formal or Informal.

Answer:

A. Information exchange or Decision making
PMBOK® Guide Reference: 4.3.2.3
Process Group: Executing
Knowledge Area: Integration

118. Project documents updated while planning risk responses include:

A. Outcomes of risks & their associated responses
B. Stakeholder tolerances & risk categories
C. Assumptions logs & change requests
D. Project schedule & stakeholder register.

Answer:

C. Assumptions logs & change requests
PMBOK® Guide Reference: 11.5.3.2
Process Group: Planning
Knowledge Area: Risk

119. Monitoring and Controlling Project Work:

A. Does not typically consume much of a project manager's time
B. Utilizes a Change Control Board (CCB)
C. Brings in project work performance data and outputs work performance information
D. Inputs project work performance information and outputs work performance reports.

Answer:

D. Inputs project work performance information and outputs work performance reports
PMBOK® Guide Reference: 4.4.1.5, 4.4.3.2
Process Group: Monitoring & Controlling
Knowledge Area: Integration

120. A key benefit of validating scope is it:

A. Identifies causes of poor processes and validates work meets stakeholder requirements
B. Brings objectivity to the customer acceptance process
C. Releases organizational resources to pursue other enterprise work
D. Documents agreements for future reference.

Answer:

B. Brings objectivity to the customer acceptance process
PMBOK® Guide Reference: A.1.7.3
Process Group: Monitoring & Controlling
Knowledge Area: Chapter 3; Scope

121. You are talking to the contractor building your new home, who was very excited to find out that you are a project manager. You have asked him why there has been no noticeable activity on the site over the last week. He just informed you that a week ago, the foundation slab was poured, and that it must cure for ten days before framing activity can begin. This predecessor-successor relationship attribute is known as:

A. Lead
B. Mandatory
C. Lag
D. Fixed.

Answer:

C. Lag
PMBOK® Guide Reference: 6.3.2.3
Process Group: Planning
Knowledge Area: Time

122. You are 4 months into a 6-month, $12,000 project with a planned linear spend. You have produced value of $8,000 and spent $9,000. Assuming you have corrected any issues causing your variances, what is your projected Variance at Completion?

A. $1,000
B. $0
C. $13,000
D. -$1,000.

Answer:

D. -$1,000 (The EAC formula used when past variance issues have been corrected is EAC = AC + BAC − EV, or $9,000 + $12,000 - $8,000, or $13,000; VAC = BAC − EAC = $12,000 - $13,000, or -$1,000)
PMBOK® Guide Reference: 7.4, Table 7-1
Process Group: Monitoring & Controlling
Knowledge Area: Cost

123. In planning procurements, which of the following would likely be used as source selection criteria?

A. Cultural fit of the seller team
B. Life cycle costs and financial capacity
C. Gender balance of the bidder team
D. Pure project cost, without regard for life cycle costs past implementation.

Answer:

B. Life cycle costs and financial capacity
PMBOK® Guide Reference: 12.1.3.4
Process Group: Planning
Knowledge Area: Procurement

124. A good project management plan (as opposed to project documents) includes:

A. A Change Management Plan
B. Project Calendars
C. Team Performance Assessments
D. A Stakeholder Register.

Answer:

A. A Change Management Plan
PMBOK® Guide Reference: 4.2.3.1, Table 4-1
Process Group: Planning
Knowledge Area: Integration

125. Your fellow PM has just stopped by your desk to chat. She sees that you are down in the dumps. When she asks why, you tell her that you're working a very labor intensive project, and struggling to organize the many types and number of resources. She suggests you use an RBS to categorize your resources hierarchically. An RBS, in this context, is a:

A. Risk Breakdown Structure
B. Resource Breakdown Structure
C. Resource Break-Fix
D. Responsibility Breakdown Structure.

Answer:

B. Resource Breakdown Structure
PMBOK® Guide Reference: 6.4.3.2
Process Group: Planning
Knowledge Area: Time

126. A project was budgeted to take 2,000 hours of work. 750 hours have been burned, and 600 hours of value have actually been created. Your SPI is .9. What is the project's SV?

A. 150
B. -150
C. 67
D. -67.

Answer:

D. -67. SV = EV – PV. EV = 600; PV = EV/SPI = 600/.9 = 667. 600 - 667 = -67.
PMBOK® Guide Reference: 6.7.2.1; Table 7-1
Process Group: Planning
Knowledge Area: Time

127. The *PMBOK® Guide* contains:

A. 47 processes, 10 knowledge areas and 5 project groups
B. 42 processes, 10 knowledge areas and 5 process groups
C. 47 processes, 10 knowledge areas and 5 process groups
D. 42 processes, 9 knowledge areas and 5 process groups.

Answer:

C. 47 processes, 10 knowledge areas and 5 process groups
PMBOK® Guide Reference: 3.9; Table 3-1
Chapter 3

128. Conditions driving the business need for a project include:

A. Solution or quality requirements
B. Market demand or legal requirements
C. Transition or operational requirements
D. Training or quality requirements.

Answer: B.
Market demand or legal requirements
PMBOK® Guide Reference: 4.1.1.2
Process Group: Initiating
Knowledge Area: Integration

129. Group Decision-Making Techniques include:

A. Plurality
B. Consensus
C. Collaboration
D. Compromise.

Answer:

A. Plurality
PMBOK® Guide Reference: 5.5.2.2
Process Group: Monitoring & Controlling
Knowledge Area: Scope

130. At the beginning of your project, you and your sponsor agreed on acceptable limits for the project's process variables. You are now 3 months into the project. The sponsor is asking you if the variables are within those limits. To answer him, you consult your:

A. Run Chart
B. Control Chart
C. Scatter Diagram
D. Histogram.

Answer:

B. Control Chart
PMBOK® Guide Reference: 8.1.2.3
Process Group: Planning
Knowledge Area: Quality

131. A Quantitative Risk Analysis technique that uses simulations and probability distributions is:

A. Sensitivity analysis
B. Expected monetary value analysis
C. Monte Carlo technique
D. Expert Judgment.

Answer:

C. Monte Carlo technique
PMBOK® Guide Reference: 11.4.2
Process Group: Planning
Knowledge Area: Risk

132. Process group interactions mean that:

A. All process groups but Initiating & Closing overlap with each other over time
B. More project budget is spent in Planning than any other process group
C. All process groups overlap with each other over time
D. More project manager time is spent in Executing processes than elsewhere.

Answer:

A. All process groups but Initiating & Closing overlap with each other over time
PMBOK® Guide Reference: 3.1 Figure 3-2
Chapter 3

133. Configuration Management activities include which of the following?

A. Making a list of changes occurring during a project
B. Making a list of potential future project impacting events
C. Configuration status accounting
D. Configuration scope creep control.

Answer:

C. Configuration status accounting
PMBOK® Guide Reference: 4.5
Process Group: Monitoring & Control
Knowledge Area: Integration

134. Major components in a contract agreement would include:

A. Constraints & assumptions
B. Traceability objectives & business rules
C. Functional & non-functional requirements
D. Penalties & incentives.

Answer:

D. Penalties & incentives
PMBOK® Guide Reference: 12.2.3.2
Process Group: Executing
Knowledge Area: Procurement

135. You have been told that a project activity will most likely take 10 days. If all goes well, it will only take 6 days. However, if Murphy's law strikes, it could take 20 days. Given this uncertainty, you have decided to estimate the activity using a Beta, or PERT, distribution. You deliver an estimate of:

A. 10 days
B. 13 days
C. 12 Days
D. 11 Days.

Answer:

D. 11 Days (Est = ((6 + 4(10) + 20)/6) = 66/6 = 11)
PMBOK® Guide Reference: 6.5.2.4
Process Group: Planning
Knowledge Area: Time

136. A type of audit that identifies nonconforming organizational/project processes is:

A. Procurement Audit
B. Quality Audit
C. Risk Audit
D. Tax Audit.

Answer:

B. Quality Audit
PMBOK® Guide Reference: 8.2.2.2
Process Group: Executing
Knowledge Area: Quality

137. Arguably the most useful tool/technique used in qualifying risk, the Probability and Impact Matrix:

A. Is used in determining risk urgency levels
B. Marries probability and impact to rate risks as high, medium or low priority
C. Is used in categorizing risks
D. Is a statistical tool utilizing probability distributions.

Answer:

B. Marries probability and impact to rate risks as high, medium or low priority
PMBOK® Guide Reference: 11.3.2.1
Process Group: Planning
Knowledge Area: Risk

138. You are exactly midway through a 6-month, $12,000 project with a planned linear spend. You have spent $4,000, and have produced value of $5,400. What is your CV?

A. -$1400
B. Not enough information to determine
C. 1.35
D. $1400.

Answer:

D. $1400 (CV = EV – AC = $5400 - $4000 = $1400)
PMBOK® Guide Reference: 7.4, Table 7-1
Process Group: Monitoring & Controlling
Knowledge Area: Cost

139. Tools and Techniques used in the Close Project or Phase Process include:

A. Analytical techniques such as regression & trend analysis
B. Procurement negotiations
C. Records management systems
D. Procurement audits.

Answer:

A. Analytical techniques such as regression & trend analysis
PMBOK® Guide Reference: 4.6.2
Process Group: Closing
Knowledge Area: Integration

140. While working in the Planning processes, you will be:

A. Writing the project charter
B. Delineating the strategy and tactics for the project
C. Guiding project team selection and assignment
D. Reviewing change requests.

B. Delineating the strategy and tactics for the project
PMBOK® Guide Reference: A.1.5
Process Group: Planning
Chapter 3

141. Organizational Process Assets Updates Outputs of the Close Project or Phase Process include which of the following?

A. Closed procurements
B. Final product, service or result transition
C. Project or phase closure documents
D. Procurement files.

Answer:

C. Project or phase closure documents
PMBOK® Guide Reference: 4.6.3
Process Group: Closing
Knowledge Area: Integration

142. You have just finished work on a document that includes a project scope statement, a WBS and a WBS dictionary. What have you just completed?

A. Performance Measurement Baseline
B. Requirements Document
C. SOW
D. Scope Baseline.

Answer:

D. Scope Baseline
PMBOK® Guide Reference: 5.4.3.1
Process Group: Planning
Knowledge Area: Scope

143. Dependency attributes include:

A. Mandatory or Discretionary
B. Fixed or Variable
C. Lead or Lag
D. PDM or ADM.

Answer:

A. Mandatory or Discretionary
PMBOK® Guide Reference: 6.3.2.2
Process Group: Planning
Knowledge Area: Time

144. Work Performance Data

A. Are measurements integrated and analyzed in context
B. Are raw observations regarding such things as completion status of deliverables
C. Are physical representations of work performance
D. Are the same as Earned Value calculations.

Answer:

B. Are raw observations regarding such things as completion status of deliverables
PMBOK® Guide Reference: 3.8
Chapter 3

145. When developing a project team, which tools might you use?

A. Networking & organizational theory
B. Negotiation & Multi-Criteria Decision Analysis
C. Team-Building activities & personnel assessment tools
D. Observation & Conversation.

Answer:

C. Team-Building activities & personnel assessment tools
PMBOK® Guide Reference: 9.3.2
Process Group: Executing
Knowledge Area: Human Resource Management

146. You are considering bidding on a project that could be a real growth stimulator for your enterprise, but your limited capital resources just won't stretch to meet the requirements. You are considering entering into a joint venture with a larger company that you have partnered with in the past, and that has better capital resources at their disposal. What type of risk response strategy is this?

A. Mitigation
B. Transference
C. Sharing
D. Enhancement.

Answer:

C. Sharing
PMBOK® Guide Reference: 11.5.2.2
Process Group: Planning
Knowledge Area: Risk

147. You are working on identifying project requirements. You decide to use a technique that enhances brainstorming with a voting process. You have chosen:

A. Idea/Mind Mapping
B. Nominal Group Technique
C. An Affinity Diagram
D. Multicriteria Decision Analysis.

Answer:

B. Nominal Group Technique
PMBOK® Guide Reference: 5.2.2.4
Process Group: Planning
Knowledge Area: Scope

148. You have decided to use the critical chain method to manage your project. Your concern is focused right now on managing three non-critical chains in your project network. You are considering:

A. Adding a project buffer to your network
B. Adding feeding buffers to the three non-critical chains
C. Managing the free float on your non-critical chains
D. Managing the total float on your non-critical chains.

Answer:

B. Adding feeding buffers to the three non-critical chains
PMBOK® Guide Reference: 6.6.2.3
Process Group: Planning
Knowledge Area: Time

149. Changes can be:

A. Corrective or Preventive
B. A planned workaround
C. Informal in nature
D. Approved by any project team member.

Answer:

A. Corrective or Preventive (A workaround is, by definition (P 567), not a planned event).
PMBOK® Guide Reference: 4.3
Process Group: Executing
Knowledge Area: Integration

150. What should you tell a "reluctant sponsor" is the key benefit of developing a charter?

A. It defines the basis of all project work
B. It gets the project off to a good, formalized start
C. It describes the project, service or result boundaries for the project
D. It identifies the focus for groups of stakeholders.

Answer:

B. It gets the project off to a good, formalized start
PMBOK® Guide Reference: A.1.4.1
Process Group: Initiating
Knowledge Area: Chapter 3; Integration

CAPM Exam Answer Key

Number	Answer	Kn Area	Number	Answer	Kn Area	Number	Answer	Kn Area
1	C	Chapter 3	51	D	Time	101	D	Cost
2	B	Integration	52	C	Chapter 3	102	A	Time
3	B	Procurement	53	A	Human Resource	103	B	Scope
4	D	Scope	54	D	Communication	104	C	Chapter 3
5	A	Procurement	55	C	Cost	105	D	Chapter 3
6	C	Risk	56	A	Procurement	106	D	Integration
7	B	Time	57	B	Risk	107	B	Stakeholder
8	D	Communication	58	A	Human Resource	108	A	Procurement
9	C	Human Resource	59	D	Integration	109	C	Risk
10	B	Cost	60	C	Chapter 3	110	B	Stakeholder
11	A	Chapter 3	61	B	Time	111	B	Communication
12	B	Time	62	A	Scope	112	D	Time
13	C	Human Resource	63	D	Stakeholder	113	A	Chapter 3
14	D	Stakeholder	64	A	Quality	114	C	Human Resource
15	A	Chapter 3	65	B	Risk	115	B	Cost
16	C	Integration	66	C	Cost	116	D	Scope
17	D	Communication	67	D	Chapter 3	117	A	Integration
18	B	Scope	68	A	Scope	118	C	Risk
19	A	Quality	69	C	Communication	119	D	Integration
20	D	Risk	70	B	Scope	120	B	Chapter 3
21	B	Procurement	71	D	Integration	121	C	Time
22	C	Cost	72	A	Human Resource	122	D	Cost
23	D	Chapter 3	73	C	Stakeholder	123	B	Procurement
24	A	Stakeholder	74	B	Quality	124	A	Integration
25	A	Time	75	A	Chapter 3	125	B	Time
26	D	Communication	76	D	Procurement	126	D	Time
27	B	Human Resource	77	B	Risk	127	C	Chapter 3
28	C	Risk	78	C	Communication	128	B	Integration
29	C	Integration	79	B	Scope	129	A	Scope
30	B	Scope	80	C	Integration	130	B	Quality
31	B	Risk	81	A	Stakeholder	131	C	Risk
32	A	Time	82	C	Time	132	A	Chapter 3
33	D	Chapter 3	83	D	Chapter 3	133	C	Integration
34	C	Scope	84	D	Human Resource	134	D	Procurement
35	B	Procurement	85	B	Cost	135	D	Time
36	A	Communication	86	D	Scope	136	B	Quality
37	C	Chapter 3	87	A	Cost	137	B	Risk
38	C	Time	88	C	Integration	138	D	Cost
39	A	Quality	89	A	Quality	139	A	Integration
40	B	Scope	90	B	Human Resource	140	B	Chapter 3
41	C	Procurement	91	D	Chapter 3	141	C	Integration
42	D	Procurement	92	A	Time	142	D	Scope
43	A	Risk	93	C	Stakeholder	143	A	Time
44	C	Integration	94	C	Procurement	144	B	Chapter 3
45	A	Chapter 3	95	D	Scope	145	C	Human Resource
46	B	Stakeholder	96	C	Stakeholder	146	C	Risk
47	C	Risk	97	B	Integration	147	B	Scope
48	D	Human Resource	98	A	Communication	148	B	Time
49	A	Quality	99	B	Human Resource	149	A	Integration
50	B	Time	100	C	Quality	150	B	Chapter 3

About the Author

With over 30 years' experience in software development, program management and project management, Mr. Tracy has managed over 100 major projects for national and international corporations and public sector entities. In the private sector, his responsibilities have ranged from software developer and development manager to project manager and project & program director, driving over $50 million in software projects annually. In the public sector, John has served as Chief Information Officer of a very large school district, directing major software, network, hardware and data center initiatives. He has also done senior level PM consulting work for public and private sector clients both domestically and internationally.

Over the past 12 years, Mr. Tracy has developed and delivered online and traditional project management training for educational and public institutions as well as private corporations. He holds Masters Degrees in Business Administration and Management Information Systems, has held continuous PMP certification since 1998, and is currently engaged in developing and delivering project management courseware and senior level consulting. His first book, "A Project Manager's Storybook (With Cases)" was published early in 2013. His second book, "PMBOK® Guide Edition Five 200-Question Sample PMP Exam®", was published in 2014.

19911378R00052